she says

Other Books by Vénus Khoury-Ghata

POETRY:

Compassion des pierres
Elle dit
Anthologie personnelle
Monologue du mort

FICTION:

Privilège des morts
La maison au bord des larmes
La maestra
Les fiancées du cap Tenès
Le moine, l'ottoman et la femme du grand argentier

Other Books by Marilyn Hacker

POETRY:

Desesperanto
First Cities: Collected Early Poems
Squares and Courtyards
Winter Numbers
Selected Poems 1965–1990
Going Back to the River
Love, Death, and the Changing of the Seasons
Assumptions
Taking Notice
Separations
Presentation Piece

TRANSLATIONS:

Here There Was Once a Country by Vénus Khoury-Ghata
A Long-Gone Sun by Claire Malroux
Edge by Claire Malroux

she says

VÉNUS KHOURY-GHATA

Translated by Marilyn Hacker

Graywolf Press
SAINT PAUL, MINNESOTA

Publication of this volume is made possible in part by a grant provided by the Minnesota State Arts Board, through an appropriation by the Minnesota State Legislature; a grant from the Wells Fargo Foundation Minnesota; and a grant from the National Endowment for the Arts. Significant support has also been provided by the Bush Foundation; Marshall Field's Project Imagine with support from the Target Foundation; the McKnight Foundation; and other generous contributions from foundations, corporations, and individuals. To these organizations and individuals we offer our heartfelt thanks.

MINNESOTA
STATE ARTS BOARD

NATIONAL
ENDOWMENT
FOR THE ARTS

A Lannan Translation Selection
Funding the translation and publication of exceptional literary works

The sequence "Elle dit" appeared in French in the collection *Elle dit*, published by Les Éditions Balland, 1999. The sequence "Les mots" appeared in French in the collection *Compassion des pierres*, published by Les Éditions de la Différence, 2001. "Pourquoi j'écris en français" was published in the journal *La Revue des deux mondes*, 2000.

Grateful acknowledgment is given to the editors of the journals in which some of these translations first appeared: *Ambit* (UK); *Cimarron Review*; *Field*; *Global City Review*; *The Gobshite Quarterly*; *The Kenyon Review*; *The Manhattan Review*; *North American Review*; *Poetry International*; *Poetry London* (UK); *Ratapallax*; *Women in French Studies*. "Autumn preceded summer by one day" also appeared in the *Yale Anthology of 20th Century French Poetry*, edited by Mary Ann Caws. The poem "Words" in the "Words" sequence was first published in *The New Yorker*.

Published by Graywolf Press
2402 University Avenue, Suite 203
Saint Paul, Minnesota 55114

www.graywolfpress.org

Published in the United States of America

ISBN 1-55597-383-3

2 4 6 8 9 7 5 3 1
First Graywolf Printing, 2003

Library of Congress Control Number: 2002111719

Cover design: Christa Schoenbrodt, Studio Haus

Cover art: Mark Oatney / Getty Images

Contents

Introduction

Vénus Khoury-Ghata's work presents a paradox that is familiar to many readers and writers who are "hyphenated" Americans: that of writing and thinking one language *through* another. In her case the two languages are Arabic and French, the first her mother (and her mother's) tongue, the second the language of her education and of her awakening to literature. Khoury-Ghata is a poet and novelist whose own career contains much of the picaresque. Born in Lebanon, near Beirut, in December 1937, in a modest milieu not expected to produce writers, still less poets, women poets least of all, she is now a Parisian of thirty years' standing, author of a dozen collections of poems and fourteen novels, who has, in the interim, traversed classes and cultures, survived a war, raised four children, and constructed a lyrical bridge between two languages, their traditions and their particular musics.

French is the language of choice for Khoury-Ghata's own writing, but she also has translated much contemporary poetry of the Arab world into French, and has been instrumental in the publication of numerous emerging Arab-language writers in France. She is also an energetic partisan of the rights of Francophone poets—Lebanese, West Indian, Quebecois, Nigerian, Vietnamese—to bring the cadences, the images, the forms of their own poetries with them into the French language, and to have this literature recognized as an essential part of the contemporary French tradition. This is a necessary continuation and broadening of the movement called "Négritude" described and embodied in the works of Léopold Sédar Senghor and Aimé Césaire, even more pertinent today when French culture is increasingly a mixture of native and ever more varied immigrant cultures. Several of the most praised contemporary French writers are of West Indian, Chinese, Belgian, Lebanese, Palestinian, Tunisian, or African origin.

But it's perhaps significant that while they are accepted as part of the literary mainstream as novelists, they tend, in general, to be "exoticized" as poets; their work not taken into consideration in overviews of poetic tendencies. This can also be seen as part of a literary landscape where even French regional specificity was, for a few generations, discouraged as contrary to the modern poetic project.

This collection brings together two of Khoury-Ghata's recent poem-sequences, "She Says/*Elle dit*," from the eponymous volume published in 1999, and "Words/*Les mots*," from *Compassion des pierres*, published in 2001, as well as an essay originally written for *La revue des deux mondes* in 2000, which examines with warmth, humor, and a drop of bitterness the situation of a poet whose imagination is perpetually in transit between languages.

While French is Khoury-Ghata's language of choice both in her work and in her daily life today, the Arabic language itself, like a distant lover or a lost country, becomes the subject of many of her poems. In a sequence from another book ("The Seven Honeysuckle Sprigs of Wisdom"), a schoolteacher "tries out" the letters of the Arabic alphabet, described as household tools, wildlife, or beasts of burden, before imposing them on the children. The poet has said that the rhythms and tropes of her poetic line are as much influenced by the sound of spoken Arabic and Arabic poetry as they are by the comparative austerity of French verse, whether in the classical alexandrine or post-Mallarméan open forms, even though it was largely literature in French, whether that of Pascal, Baudelaire, or her Francophone Lebanese compatriot Georges Schéhadé, which fixed her determination to write and her confidence to carry her project through. Her line follows the cadences of her story, rather than either a fixed or internal meter, a unit of breath, or placement within the white space of the page. She does not hesitate to pick up a motif, image, or key phrase out of one poem to use in another.

There is little "figurative language" in Khoury-Ghata's poetry: a few elaborate similes ("the days are like conceited generals / the nights like flashy women"; "a book / with lines which ran from east to west like Siberian trains"; "He upends her like a wineskin to drink her in one gulp") but no metaphors. Although we are in a lyrical rather than a linear narrative space, in which time is at once collapsed and extended, we are also encouraged to take the surreal elements as given, not as representing something other than themselves (which is of course the essence of surrealism). This connects her work with a tradition that is much more French than Arabic, in literature and in painting, though Khoury-Ghata's surrealism and its dominant tropes seem entirely her own, organic, with the logic of fables and fairy tales, eschewing the philosophically willed disruptions of European Surrealism.

Her most recent collection of poetry, *Compassion des pierres,* opens with the sequence called *"Les mots"*—"Words" (translated here)— which creates a mythology of words, or "the word": not the words of French or Arabic, but of all languages, a myth of speech and of writing created simultaneously by human beings and by the natural world of which they are a part. In her dawn of origins, words issue from and belong to birds, to stones, to the night sky:

I'll tell you everything there were five pebbles
one for each continent
vast enough   to contain a child of a different color

pebbles which:

    broke up into alphabets
ate a different earth   on each continent

Her fable of origins continues with the letters of the Arabic, the Roman, the Cyrillic alphabet contrasted with those unknown antediluvian alphabets,

                      which didn't survive the
rising of the waters   letters buried in their silicate vestments
become silenced sounds in the silenced silt

Just as Khoury-Ghata's verbal imagination of the word, sentence, and poetic line and her balance of sound and sense function fluidly between two languages, so does her writerly perception travel fluidly between genres: poetry and fiction, with a constant intercourse between the two. Khoury-Ghata is an inveterate storyteller—even in conversation, the account of a trip to the flea market at the Porte de

Clignancourt with her daughter or of a trip to Sénégal with an international writers' delegation becomes a multileveled tale with detailed descriptions of character and landscape, merciless satire of every kind of officiousness, and unexpected asides that recoup and connect—indeed, the flea market to the writers' congress. When her anecdotes deal with the past, the listener never knows if the end of the story will be someone's personal victory over obstacles—poverty, war, illness—or an act of violence, an unanticipated death. Her novels range from the historical picaresque (five Frenchwomen shipwrecked on the Algerian coast in 1802; a Trinitarian monk sent to bring back a dignitary's wife eloped with a Syrian merchant) to the familial (her own brother's descent from emerging poet to drug addict silenced by electroshock in war-wracked Beirut) to the fantastic (a widow's return to a Mediterranean island where the dead cohabit with the living). They almost always deal, in some fashion, with a passage between Europe and the Middle East, and with the passage, equally two-way, between life and death. Her poems, composed for the most part in sequences, often have the quality of exploded narratives, reassembled in a mosaic in which the reader has at least the illusion of being able to find a more linear connecting thread. But in the end, it is the design of the mosaic itself that is most memorable. The same themes that animate the fiction are predominant in the poems: the tension between movement/change and tradition/sources, with all that is positive and negative in both; the unceasing commerce between human beings and the rest of the natural world, and between the dead and the living; the independent, puissant, and transcultural life of words.

In the poems as in the novels, there is often the figure of a woman (or of "woman") as tenacious survivor, mourner, interpreter and translator for the most unlikely interlocutors, perpetual bilingual. In one book-length sequence, "*Basse Enfance*" ("Early Childhood" but with the added implication of "low" as in class or suppression: a contrast with the more usual expression "*haute enfance*," which simply means preadolescence), the figure is that of the poet's mother, whom she elsewhere describes as "illiterate in two languages," at once homebound, afraid of her children's vagrant imaginations, and a tireless force not stopped by sleep or death. Here, in "She Says," the oracular female figure is more ambiguous. She is linked, again and again, with trees—the larch, the cherry, the sycamore, the fig tree, as well as the clinging wisteria—with whom she holds contentious debates; there is a soldier in her memory who reminds her of a war she would rather forget, of bombed buildings and displaced children; there is an angel who does household chores; there are the dead, who arrive like importunate relatives at her door. Wolves are among her familiars. She is linked, of course, with words, from the title, which privileges her speech, and which occurs like a refrain through the sequence, to the numerous depictions of the act of writing and reading: her pen dipped into an inkwell of lamentations, her book sown into a shroud, she writes as she dreams, "in parallel slashes that meet beyond the page." "She" is a woman who has seized the word, written and spoken, that overrules even the laws of geometry. But she is also at a point of electric stasis between enclosure and departure, between a house loud with contrapuntal histories and a world beyond inhabited by the familiar trees, wolves, caravans, and constellations, but where the hints of destruction and exile are insistent. She is not visibly a mother or a daughter, a lover, spouse, or comrade, though sometimes she seems to be in mourning. She has the stature of a mythological figure, Antigone or Bérénice, Deborah or Fatima, but she comes from the author's own frame of reference, from her own annals of myth, which here are neither European nor Middle Eastern but self-created, as this poet has, indeed, invented herself, and produced a body of work from a synthesis of multiple traditions and a unique imagination.

Marilyn Hacker
Paris, 2002

she says

Les Mots

Words

Les mots   je le sais maintenant   déclamaient du vent à l'époque
à part les cailloux il y avait des lunes mais pas de lampes
les étoiles sortirent plus tard d'une empoignade entre deux silex

Cinq cailloux pour tout vous dire
un par continent
assez vaste   pour contenir un enfant de couleur différente

Il y avait donc   cinq enfants mais pas de maisons
des fenêtres mais pas de murs
du vent mais pas de rues
le premier homme portait une pierre autour du cou

Il fit un arrangement avec le premier arbre
un chêne si mes souvenirs sont bons
celui qui arrivait avant l'autre buvait l'océan

Le langage en ce temps-là était une ligne droite réservée aux oiseaux
la lettre "i" fente de colibri femelle
"h" échelle à une seule marche nécessaire pour remplacer avant la
      nuit un soleil grillé
"o" trou dans la semelle de l'univers

Contrairement aux consonnes aux vêtements rêches
les voyelles étaient nues
tout l'art du tissage consistait à ménager leur susceptibilité
le soir elles se comptaient entre elles pour s'assurer qu'aucune ne
      manquait
dans les pays caillouteux les hommes avaient un sommeil sans rêves

In those days   I know now   words declaimed the wind
besides pebbles there were moons but no lamps
the stars would emerge later from a brawl between two flintstones

I'll tell you everything there were five pebbles
one for each continent
vast enough   to contain a child of a different color

So there were   five children but no houses
windows but no walls
wind but no streets
the first man wore a stone around his neck

He made an arrangement with the first tree
an oak if I remember correctly
the one who got there first could drink up the ocean

Language at that time was a straight line reserved for birds
the letter "i" was the cleft of a female hummingbird
"h" a ladder with one rung necessary to replace a charred sun before
     nightfall
"o" a hole in the sole of the universe

Unlike the consonants with their rough garments
the vowels were naked
all the weaver's art consisted of humoring them
in the evening they counted each other to make sure no one was
     missing
in the rocky countries men slept without dreaming

Les mots
vol aveugle dans les ténèbres
lucioles tournoyant sur elles-mêmes
cailloux dans la poche du mort distrait
projectiles contre le mur du cimetière
ils se disloquent en alphabets
mangent une terre différente   dans chaque continent.

Aleph souffle de droite à gauche
pour effacer dunes et chameliers
qui comptent les étoiles la tête dans le sable
douze fois de suite
Ainsi

C'est dans la bassine du "Ba"   qu'on lave le sang menstruel de la
    lune
dans le cuivre pérenne
quand les femmes sur les terrasses nocturnes   font des vœux
    irréfléchis

"Tah" arpente une terre pauvre en herbe et en compassion
seules comptent les gesticulations de l'ombre qui
efface   écrit
efface   écrit pas et passants

Il y a des alphabets de ville et des alphabets de champ
Dis-moi quels mots tu emploies je te dirai   le nombre de tes bovins

Words
blind flight in the darkness
fireflies wheeling in on themselves
pebbles in the pocket of an absentminded dead man
projectiles against the cemetery wall
they broke up into alphabets
ate a different earth   on each continent.

Aleph breathes from right to left
to erase dunes and camel drivers
who count the stars with their heads in the sand
twelve times in a row
Thus

It's in "Ba's" basin   that the moon's menstrual blood is washed
in the eternal copper
when women on nocturnal terraces   make rash vows

"Tah" paces up and down land poor in grass and compassion
all that counts are the gesticulations of the shadow which
erases   writes
erases   writes steps and passersby

There are country alphabets and town alphabets
Tell me what words you use I'll tell you   the number of your cattle

D'où viennent les mots?
de quel frottement de sons sont-ils nés
à quel silex allumaient-ils leur mèche
quels vents les ont convoyés jusqu'à nos bouches

Leur passé est bruissement de silences retenus
barrissement de matières en fusion
grognement d'eaux mauvaises

Parfois
Ils s'étrécissent en cri
se dilatent en lamentations
deviennent buée sur les vitres des maisons mortes
se cristallisent pépites de chagrin sur les lèvres mortes
se fixent sur une étoile déchue
creusent leur trou dans le rien
aspirent les âmes égarées

Les mots sont des larmes pierreuses
les clés des portes initiales
ils maugréaient dans les cavernes
prêtaient leur vacarme aux tempêtes
leur silence au pain enfourné vivant

Where do words come from?
from what rubbing of sounds are they born
on what flint do they light their wicks
what winds brought them into our mouths

Their past is the rustling of stifled silences
the trumpeting of molten elements
the grunting of stagnant waters

Sometimes
they grip each other with a cry
expand into lamentations
become mist on the windows of dead houses
crystallize into chips of grief on dead lips
attach themselves to a fallen star
dig their hole in nothingness
breathe out strayed souls

Words are rocky tears
the keys to the first doors
they grumble in caverns
lend their ruckus to storms
their silence to bread that's ovened alive

Comment trouver le nom du pêcheur qui ferra le premier mot
de la femme qui le réchauffa sous son aisselle
ou de celle qui le prenant pour un caillou le lança sur un chien errant?

que savons-nous des alphabets de sable enfouis sous les pieds des
    caravanes
devenus silice
éclats de verre
vénérés par les chameliers comme débris d'étoile?

Faut-il interroger les dénudeurs des dunes
les vents   sans foi ni loi   qui déterrent les ossements
puis jettent leur craie   à la lune qui blanchit le tendre et le sec
ou feuilleter les strates des falaises à la recherche du chasseur UN
qui visa au lance-pierres le premier chiffre
l'enferma dans une cage
et lui apprit à chanter jusqu'à dix

Son chant alluma la première bougie
C'est à la flamme que nous devons les premières superstitions:
"Trois bougies alignés annoncent une dispute"
"Quatre cierges autour d'une couche appellent la mort"

Chasseur et pêcheur étaient fixes à l'époque
seul le temps marchait
celui qui n'aimait pas mourir enfermait un soleil dans son puits
la fortune d'un homme s'évaluait au nombre de ses ouvertures
une touffe de genêt surmontait la caverne du notable
sa vie se mesurait par le nombre de femmes enrobées de son odeur
sa poussière le dit

How to find the name of the fisherman who hooked the first word
of the woman who warmed it in her armpit
or of the one who mistook it for a pebble and threw it at a stray dog?

what do we know of the alphabets of sand buried beneath the feet of
    caravans
turned into silica
shards of glass
venerated by the camel drivers as star-debris?

Must we question those who strip the dunes
those winds   lawless and faithless   which unearth men's bones
then throw their chalk   at the moon which bleaches the tender and
    the dry
must we leaf through the cliffs' layers in search of the FIRST hunter
who fired the first number at a stone-thrower
shut him up in a cage
and taught him how to sing up to ten

His song lit the first candle
It's to that flame that we owe the first superstitions:
"Three lit candles mean there'll be a quarrel"
"Four tapers around a bed call death down"

Hunter and fisherman were rooted at that time
only time walked
those who didn't like dying shut a sun up in their wells
a man's fortune was measured by the number of his openings
a tuft of broom grew over the dignitary's cave
his life was measured by the number of women wrapped in his odor
his dust says so

L'homme prudent accrochait sa famille à sa ceinture
la mode le voulait
la lune n'était qu'un réflexe du soleil qui plongeait deux fois de suite
    dans le même puits
la première pour se laver
la deuxième pour déplacer son poids d'eau et de bruit
le froid l'étrécissait aux dimensions d'une pomme
se hisser sur la pointe des pieds suffisait pour le cueillir
l'été le dilatait d'un horizon à l'autre
le ciel était son hamac renversé

Soleil était le nom du premier coq
lune celui de la première poule
le pain à portée de main de la lune   disparaissait selon le chasseur
son coq devenu aphone
il se désintéressa du calendrier
le temps s'écrivit alors au brouillon
on tirait les années à courte paille
la nuit   le jour se jouaient à pile ou face
le basilic décidait de tout

The prudent man looped his family to his belt
that was the fashion
the moon was only a reflex of the sun which dived into the same well
    twice
the first time to wash itself
the second time to displace its weight of water and noise
the cold squeezed it to the size of an apple
one could pluck it merely by standing on tiptoe
summer stretched it from one horizon to another
the sky was its hammock turned upside down

Sun was the name of the first rooster
moon that of the first hen
bread within the moon's reach disappeared   according to the hunter
his rooster gone hoarse
he lost interest in the calendar
then time was written in a rough draft
they drew straws for the years
night   and day tossed a coin heads or tails
the basil decided everything

Le langage en ce temps-là faisait feu de tout bruit
Il arpentait les pâturages à la recherche de pousses sonores qu'il
    broutait de droite à gauche par ordre d'intonations
Jamais plus d'un pâturage avant la grande transhumance sur les
    sommets de l'alphabet où le parler se fait rare

L'odeur sucrée du chèvrefeuille attirait les lettres juvéniles et les
    abeilles

B revenait la bouche barbouillée de mûres
F titubait à force d'avoir fumé l'herbe du diable
son échelle sur le dos H prétendait avoir escaladé le mur du son

Dans les pays froids les lettres mâles étaient poilues
L'eau était la méditation de la terre
sa pensée intime divulguée au grand jour
son parler caillouteux
Le ruisseau se lisait à voix haute
la mer répétait la même phrase de continent à continent

Il y avait des mots à cornes et à plumes
et des mots convenablement vêtus
nus étaient ceux chassés du paradis parce qu'ils manquèrent de pudeur
Ils errent à la recherche d'un miroir où pénétrer avec l'approbation
    du tain
leur présence est signalée par un tremblement de la lumière
par un cliquetis de verre lorsqu'ils s'alignent sur les rambardes des
    fenêtres
les enfants peureux les appellent les vitreurs
On se marie avec les mots de sa langue
pour se stabiliser
les voyages c'est pour les autres
qui empruntent les lignes comme on prend le train

Language at that time opened fire on every noise
It paced up and down the pastures in search of sound-sprouts on
    which it grazed from right to left in order of their intonations
Never more than one pasture before the great seasonal migration to
    the peaks of the alphabet where speech is rare

The sugared odor of the honeysuckle attracted young letters and bees

B came back with its mouth bearded with blackberries
F was staggering from having smoked devil's weed
its ladder on its back, H pretended to have scaled the sound barrier

In cold countries the male letters were hairy
Water was the earth's meditation
its intimate thoughts revealed in the light of day
its pebbly dialect
The stream read itself out loud
the sea repeated the same sentence from continent to continent

There were words with horns and feathers
and properly dressed words
those driven from paradise for their lack of modesty were naked
They wandered in search of a mirror they could penetrate with its
    silvering's approval
their presence was signaled by a trembling of the light
by a jangling of glass when they lined up on the windows' guardrails
timid children call them the glassy ones
One marries the words of one's own language
to settle down
traveling is for the others
who borrow lines the way they take a train

Que savons-nous des alphabets qui n'ont pas résisté à la montée des
    eaux   des lettres enfouies dans leur vêtement de silice   devenues
    sons éteints dans la vase éteinte
que savons-nous de "Aïn" qui allumait sa lampe entre deux vagues
    de la concavité matricielle de "noun"   de la putrescibilité de
    "Ha"   de la pesanteur légendaire de "Tah"

C'est dans un linceul à quatre nœuds   dans un filet de pierre
    qu'Aleph fut repêchée au large de TYR la vieille car seul le varech
    parlait   à l'époque   le silence blanchissait les murs
"Dad" est ma mère dit la terre
"Sad" ma marâtre
Elles marchent depuis le début de l'alphabet à la recherche de la lettre
    UNE qu'on soulève telle dalle de pierre pour retrouver les
    ossements de la langue première   celle grommelée par des lèvres
    devenues friables à force de frotter leur voix sur le silex

"Aleph"   baguette de sourcier
va-nu-pieds traduit en sept langues
bâton pour dresser les chats et donner au plus chaste la cage du colibri

"Sine"   louche percée
qui repêche les étoiles dans la bassine de confitures du diable

"Ra"   appelle à son secours les anges qui
traversent l'évangile à pied

"Kaf"   lettre criarde qui
sème la zizanie entre les tribus
son pied bot charrie de vieilles colères   venues d'un lointain alphabet

What do we know about the alphabets which didn't survive the rising
    of the waters   letters buried in their silicate vestments   become
    silenced sounds in the silenced silt
what do we know about "Aïn" which lit its lamp between two waves
    about the womblike concavity of "noun"   of the putrescibility
    of "Ha"   of the legendary weight of "Tah"

It was in a quadruple-knotted shroud   in a net of stone   that
    Aleph was fished up offshore from the old city of TYR because
    only the kelp spoke   at that time   silence whitened the walls
"Dad" is my mother said the earth
"Sad" is my stepmother
They walked from the beginning of the alphabet in search of the
    letter ONE which they lifted like a gravestone to find the remains
    of the first language   the one mumbled by lips become crumbly
    from rubbing their voices against the flintstone

"Aleph"   a magician's wand
a tramp translated into seven languages
a stick to train cats with and give the hummingbird's cage to the
    chastest one

"Sine"   a slotted ladle
that scoops up stars from the bowl where the devil makes marmalade

"Ra"   calls for help to the angels
who cross the Gospels on foot

"Kaf"   a gaudy letter which
sows discord among the tribes
its club foot drags along old angers   come from a faraway alphabet

Les mots qui poussent en bordure des lèvres retiennent bien des
    frayeurs
les enfants les font sécher entre les pages
tête-bêche comme les roses foulées par les colombes
le sang qui bat à leur tempe désole les mères qui essorent les murs
    après les pluies

les livres   disent-elles   s'attristent sans raison
ils veulent des mots secs alors que la saison est mouillée
l'humidité rétrécit les maisons et fait pleurer le linge

The words which spring up on the borders of lips retain their terrors
children dry them between the pages
head-to-tail like roses trodden by doves
the blood beating in their temples grieves the mothers who dry the
    walls out after the rains

books   the mothers say   become sad for no reason
they want dry words when it's the rainy season
the dampness shrinks houses and makes the laundry weep

Les mots, dit-elle, étaient des loups
ils s'alignaient sur les cimes pour raconter à la lune la difficulté du vent
    à escalader la pente
la suffisance des troupeaux
et les mouvements chaotiques des nuages transhumants

Ils déposaient leur colère à ses pieds quand elle tournait le livre noir de
    la nuit   s'endormaient dans les élucubrations des pages qui
    parlaient d'un pays   doré à la feuille où le sommeil   tombe
    dans les puits avec sa charge d'étoiles enturbannées
Mais les loups   ne connaissaient pas l'Orient

Words, she says, used to be wolves
they lined up on the mountain peaks to tell the moon about the
    difficulty of climbing the slope
the complacency of the flocks
and the chaotic movements of migrating clouds

They placed their anger at the moon's feet when it turned the black
    book of night   went to sleep amidst the ranting of the pages
    which spoke of a gold-leafed country   where sleep   drops
    into the wells with its load of turbaned stars
But wolves   don't know the Orient

Les mots, dit-elle, c'est comme la pluie   tout le monde sait en
    fabriquer
il suffit d'essorer un nuage de travers pour que Noé écrive des deux
    mains
Il pleut pour apprendre à compter aux réverbères
pour semer la zizanie entre les pigeons
hérisser la peau du linge sur les cordes

Il pleut pour pleuvoir
et faire croire aux morts que la mer a déménagé plus haut

Contrairement au vent qui parle en son propre nom
la pluie a son porte-parole   le brouillard muet
si seulement chaque homme avait sa gouttière pour pouvoir discuter
    à travers les nuages avec Dieu

Words, she says, are like the rain   everyone knows how to make
    them
you only have to wring a cloud out upside down and Noah will
    write with both hands
It rains to teach the streetlights how to count
to sow disorder among the pigeons
raise the hackles of the laundry hung on clotheslines

It rains to rain
and make the dead think that the sea has moved to a higher place

Unlike the wind which speaks for itself
the rain has a spokesman   the mute fog
if only every man had his own drainpipe to discuss things with God
    through the clouds

C'est là et nulle part ailleurs
sur une terre ceinturée par les vents
que les premiers mots discutèrent d'un problème d'eau et d'une place
    au soleil

la bouche remplie de vacarme
ils racontèrent les poussières muettes et les cris des rochers

leur nombre n'excédait pas celui des vivants
un mot par homme
celui qui mourait cédait   sa place à l'arbre de son choix

Homme et chêne partageaient la même écorce
le même âge inscrit dans l'aubier
et même ombre
l'arbre en haut
l'homme en bas
et parfois l'inverse quand il prenait à la terre l'envie de se retourner

It was there and nowhere else
on an earth girdled with winds
that the first words discussed the problems of water and a place in the
    sun

their mouths filled with blaring
they told of the mute dust and the cries of the rocks

their number was no greater than that of the living
one man one word
a man who died gave up   his place to the tree of his choice

Man and oak shared the same bark
the same age inscribed in the sapwood
and the same shadow
the tree above
the man below
and sometimes the other way around when the earth felt like turning
    over

La pluie avait peu d'adeptes à l'époque
les gouttières ne canalisaient que des rumeurs
et les bassines sur les toits recueillaient la sueur des étoiles

Fatiguées de tordre un linge sec
les femmes s'appuyaient sur l'air comme au bars d'un fiancé

les maisons avaient perdu leurs portes avec leurs illusions
celui qui s'engouffrait   par une brèche   gagnait une paire d'ailes
  et une paire de ciseaux

on affûtait la mariée pour l'introduire dans le sommeil de l'homme
l'enfant né de leur accouplement avait des mains de laine en
  prévision de la neige à venir
une neige qui sortirait du sol
tout un peuple fixait ses orteils

The rain had few followers at that time
the gutterspouts ran only with rumors
and the troughs on the rooftops collected the sweat of the stars

Tired of wringing out dry laundry
women leaned on the air as on a sweetheart's arm

the houses had lost their doors along with their illusions
anyone who'd rush   in through a gap in the wall   won a pair of
    wings and a pair of scissors

they'd sharpen the bride to needle her into the man's sleep
the child born of their coupling had woolen hands in anticipation of
    the coming snow
a snow which would come up through the ground
a whole people's toes planted there

Coupables d'oublis répétés   les mots se retirèrent sur les terres froides pour subir l'épreuve du silence et se châtier d'avoir dépassé leur sens dans une langue qui n'admet pas les débordements

Ils vécurent dans un silence blanc   chassèrent des sons inaudibles pêchèrent les remous des marécages boueux

leur forme variait avec la lumière   Le soir qui estompe les angles les transformait en objets peureux

Tassés au pied des murs ils guettaient le sommeil qui leur assignait leur place dans les rêves

le sommeil de l'herboriste était peuplé d'aloès

les ermites en faisaient des décoctions qu'ils buvaient front contre terre

Guilty of repeated forgetfulness   words retreated over the cold
    ground to endure the ordeal of silence and punishment for having
    overflowed their meanings in a language which admits no excesses
They lived in a white silence   hunted inaudible sounds   fished in
    the eddies of muddy marshes
their form changed with the light   The evening which smoothed
    out angles transformed them into timid objects
Crammed together against the foot of the wall they watched for sleep
    which would find a place for them in dreams
the herbalist's sleep was peopled with aloes
hermits made brews of it which they drank with their foreheads
    pressed to the earth

Il est des mots de jardins pauvres qui croisent le fer avec les ronces
Des mots d'origines obscures qui sont l'ordinaire des morts   Les
soleils rapides leur envoient des baisers jaunes   L'if silencieux les
détourne des abeilles   Mots incolores   qui dorment dans les
huches avec le consentement du pain   se réveillent avec
les miroirs   revêtent leur écho s'aventurent dans les villes
traversent les bouches sans regarder   boitent des deux pieds
pourrissent au contact des lèvres   terminent leur parcours dans
le caniveau avec les lunes qui ont épuisé toute leur réserve
d'allumettes

There are words from poor people's gardens that crossbreed iron and
thorns   Words of obscure origins which is the usual lot of words
Swift suns send them yellow kisses   The silent yew chases the
bees away from them   Colorless words   that sleep in the
breadbox with the bread's consent   wake up with the mirrors
dress up their echoes   venture into the cities   cross mouths
without looking both ways   limp on both feet   rot at the
touch of lips   finish their journey in the gutter with the moons
which have used up all their matches

Elle Dit

She Says

Il y avait trop de femmes pour très peu de saisons
certaines se convertissaient en saule pour balayer les fleuves
Un village sans issue
les secrets des habitants s'affichaient aux battants des portes
l'odeur des épouses manipulées dans l'obscurité imprégnait les murs
Aucune pluie ne pouvait l'effacer

Les femmes existaient par leur senteur
et les hommes devaient les chercher dans les pliures des draps
dans les relents du sang lavé dans les cuivres

Les travaux mensuels étaient leur lot
elles frottaient jusqu'à l'usure les toits souillés par les déjections de la
    lune
et par les menstrues des cigognes pubères

Il paraît que l'arc-en-ciel est né là
de la pluie qui précéda Noé
une pluie sèche qui ruissela en cailloux en galets

Alors tout était blanc
l'herbe les yeux des enfants ceux des lapins

For Pierre Brunel

There were too many women for too few seasons
some of them turned themselves into willows to sweep the rivers
A dead-end village
the inhabitants' secrets were posted on swinging doors
the scent of wives handled in darkness impregnated the walls
No rain could erase it

The women existed through their fragrance
and the men had to search for them in the folds of sheets
in the stink of blood washed in copper pots

Monthly labor was the women's lot
they scrubbed at roofs soiled by the moon's excretions
and the menstrual blood of pubescent storks
till they wore the roof-tiles down

It appears that the rainbow was born there
of the rain which came before Noah
a dry rain which dripped pebbles and small stones

And then everything was white
the grass children's eyes the eyes of rabbits

Elle dit
creuse là où l'ombre peut se tenir debout
Et elle ferme sa porte aux arbres venus partager son deuil

L'odeur douceâtre du chèvrefeuille flotte sur la rue
et annonce le cercueil porté par un seul homme

La morte a l'âge du bougainvillier de sa fenêtre
Le hennissement d'un cheval fait claquer ses volets

Chagrin vaste comme le jardin
plus hermétique que la cage du canari
Le jardinier porte son échelle telle une croix de dimanche
son sécateur coupe avec les mêmes gestes les branches
et la mèche du souvenir

Sur la vitre
ses larmes se teignent en rouge sous le dernier soleil

She says
dig there where a shadow can stand upright
And she closes her door on the trees come to share her mourning

The sugary smell of honeysuckle floats over the street
and announces the coffin borne by just one man

The dead woman is as old as the bougainvillea at her window
The whinnying of a horse makes the shutter clatter

Grief as vast as the garden
as hermetic as the canary's cage
On Sundays the gardener bears his ladder like a cross
his shears cut branches with the same movement
as they cut a lock of memory

On the windowpane
her tears are dyed red beneath the last sun

À Jean-Guy Pilon

Le vent dans le figuier se tait lorsqu'elle parle
et parle lorsqu'elle se tait
Jadis
elle se disputait avec un vieux
se querellait avec des chiens
faisait du troc avec un rémouleur
Le lit et la salière peuvent en témoigner
non l'armoire
gardienne muette du linge

Elle hurle pour effrayer sa voix et faire frémir l'eau de la bassine
chasse les busards pour voir leurs cris rouges déclencher l'orage
renverse le contenu du tiroir pour entendre s'invectiver couteaux et
    fourchettes

Courir jusqu'à la route ne sert qu'à son ombre
les pluies ont effacé les terres
et la planète qui tourne sur elle-même la ramènera à son point de
    départ

L'écho elle le sait n'est pas son ami
et la montagne cache une deuxième montagne plus vieille
et qui ne fera pas un signe à la femme qui discute à perdre haleine
    avec un arbre

For Jean-Guy Pilon

The wind in the fig tree quiets down when she speaks
and speaks up when she's silent
Once upon a time
she argued with an old man
quarreled with dogs
bartered with a knife-grinder
The bed and the saltshaker can attest to it
not the wardrobe
mute guardian of linens

She howls to frighten her own voice and make the water in the pond
    shudder
chases hawks to see their red cries unleash a storm
dumps out a drawer to hear the knives and forks swear at each other

To run up to the road is only good for her shadow
the rains have erased the fields
and the planet turning on itself will bring her back to her point of
    departure

She knows the echo is no friend of hers
and the mountain hides another, older mountain
which wouldn't greet a woman who talks to a tree till she's out of
    breath

Elle n'ouvre qu'aux vents qui libèrent les morts épinglés sur son
    miroir pour les enterrer plus haut dans un trou de l'air

La falaise dit-elle s'émiette comme un pain pauvre et ce ne sont pas
    les chênes taciturnes qui sauveront la réputation du paysage

Elle dit aussi qu'il suffit d'attendre la cinquième saison pour que ses
    morts lui reviennent larmes doucereuses sur les joues du pommier

Ils chevaucheront le brouillard
chevaucheront les chiens
souilleront le palier
pour exprimer leur désapprobation

Interroger les calendes complique le parcours du soleil hébergé dans
    son poulailler depuis que ses poules pondent dans le fleuve

Maudits les seuils qui ne savent pas ramasser les pas répète-t-elle
    jusqu'à l'ivresse
maudits les doigts qui transforment le pain en chagrin
maudite l'eau bue qui tourne au gel

Sa longue cohabitation avec la montagne lui apprit que les oiseaux
    migrent de nuit pour ignorer que le chemin est long

She only opens her door to the winds who liberate the dead pinned
    to her mirror to bury them higher up in a hole in the air

The cliff she says is crumbling like a poor man's bread and it's not
    those taciturn oaks which will save the landscape's reputation

She says too that she only has to wait for the fifth season for her dead
    to come back to her honeyed tears on the apple tree's cheeks

They'll stride across the fog
mount the dogs
soil the hallway
to express their disapproval

Questioning the calends complicates the route of the sun lodged in her
    chicken house since the hens began laying their eggs in the river

Curses on thresholds that don't know how to gather footsteps she
    repeats until she's drunk with it
curses on hands that turn bread into grief
curses on water which changes to frost when you drink it

Her long cohabitation with the mountain taught her that birds
    migrate at night so they won't know the road is long

Entre ses deux fenêtres un miroir
où par temps de brume et de paysage absent
elle capte des débris de visages qu'elle recolle en tenant
compte de la sape du tain

Visages anciens
Il faut chercher leurs contours sur les stèles
leurs voix dans le platane qui connaît le miroir de dos
et qui n'a pas fini d'observer leurs déplacements entre maison debout
    et maison renversée
incapable d'éclaircir les liens qui les unissent
Il retient son souffle lorsqu'il les voit enjamber les champs
pénétrer le miroir à reculons
s'y bousculer
se disputer la surface polie qui détient un peu de leur âme

Revanche sur les berceaux
retrouvailles tant de fois différées avec leur odeur
stratégie pour occuper l'espace avec le rien

Between her two windows is a mirror
in which in times of mist and absent landscape
she captures the debris of faces which she glues back together
taking into account what's leaked into the silvering

Ancient faces
She must look for their silhouettes in stelae
their voices in the plane tree which knows the mirror from behind
and which isn't done with watching their movements between the
    house that's standing and the toppled one
unable to clarify the ties that connect them
It holds its breath when it sees them step over the fields
penetrate the mirror backwards
push and shove each other there
arguing over the polished surface that's holding a bit of their souls

A revenge taken on cradles
reunions so often deferred with their odor
strategy for occupying space with emptiness

Pour André Brincourt

Sans la glycine
le jardin aurait enjambé la clôture pour s'installer sur le côté noble du
    chemin

Elle est son garde-fou contre les dérapages
sa ceinture de félicité
sa conseillère pour trier les chats et céder au plus chaste la cage du
    canari

Sans glycine
il n'y aurait plus d'automnes
mais des hivers avec des parapluies qui se croisent sans échanger une
    seule goutte de pluie

Elle s'aplatit quand les anges la traversent en coup de vent
un pot de confiture sous l'aile
et sur l'épaule le pain de la douleur

Without the wisteria
the garden would have climbed over the fence to move in on the
    posh side of the road

The wisteria is its guardrail against drifting
its belt of happiness
its counselor in judging cats and ceding the canary's cage to the
    chastest of them

Without wisteria
there would be no more autumns
only winters with umbrellas which pass each other without
    exchanging the slightest raindrop

The wisteria flattens out when angels cross it in a gust of wind
a pot of jam under each wing
and on their shoulders the bread of grief

Le pain ivre sur la table
le sel de la discorde face à l'âtre
tout est prêt pour les accueillir
et la femme qui ne fait pas confiance à sa lanterne
a libéré les lucioles

Les silhouettes encadrées par deux lunes dessinent des flèches noires
    sur la haie

À leur droite coule le cimetière blanc
à leur gauche le cimetière rouge

Ils marchent par groupes de deux
plutôt en file indienne
séparément puisqu'ils ne sont qu'un
un seul homme brouillé à mort avec son feu

"Chevauche un tilleul pour rentrer chez toi" lui crie-t-elle en
    désignant l'arbre

Drunken bread on the table
the salt of discord facing the hearth
everything is ready to welcome them
and the woman who doesn't trust her lantern
has set the fireflies free

Shapes framed by two moons draw black arrows on the hedge

On their right flows the white cemetery
and the red cemetery flows on their left

They walk two by two
more or less Indian file
separately because they are only one
a single man muddled to death with his fire

"Climb on a lime tree to go back home" she cries out to him
    pointing to the tree

À l'étage sombre de ses rêves
il y a ce soc qui laboure le sol de sa maison allant de l'évier au lit
où femmes et chattes mettent bas au grand soulagement du canari qui
    ébruite les naissances

Le même soc s'émiette sous le figuier depuis que les bras de l'homme
    se sont rouillés

Décaper le mort et ses outils est au-dessus de ses forces
décembre est plus long que l'hiver
et la pluie qui tombe sur la pluie l'empêche de s'incliner dans son
    sommeil

Hé toi!
appelle-t-elle aux heures des repas la silhouette invisible
inclinée sur le sillon
car il arrive aux morts de se pencher

On the dark landing of her dreams
there is that ploughshare which furrows the floor of her house going
    from the sink to the bed
where women and cats whelp to the great relief of the canary who
    announces births

The same ploughshare flakes away beneath the fig tree since the
    man's arms rusted

Scraping clean the dead man and his tools is beyond her strength
December is longer than the whole winter
and rain falling upon rain keeps her from bending over in her sleep

You there!
she calls out at mealtimes to the invisible silhouette
leaning over the furrow
because the dead do sometimes bend

Le gel cette année-là fendilla le dedans et le dehors
Ceux du nord n'arrivaient plus à écrire le temps
le soleil qui leur tenait lieu d'horloge avait perdu son cerceau

Ils parlaient une langue blanche lorsqu'ils s'aventuraient sur les pierres
nommaient sept objets admis par le feu
sept outils contondants
sept herbes pour nourrir un mort familier

La main en visière sur le front
ils croyaient lire une hirondelle
mais ce n'était que caillou gelé et froissement de plumes tombant à
     pieds joints

Avril n'améliora pas leur ordinaire
L'herbe du diable arrachée
ils mangèrent une terre si froide que leurs dents devinrent diaphanes

Cent soleils promenés au bout d'un fil n'effacèrent pas les visages pris
     dans le gel
Ils accusèrent à tort la configuration des murs
alors qu'une lune mauvaise avait craché dans leurs miroirs

The frost that year shattered both the indoors and outdoors
The northerners couldn't write down what time it was
the sun which served as their clock had lost its hoop

They spoke a white language when they ventured onto the rocks
named seven objects tolerated by fire
seven blunt tools
seven herbs to feed a dead man in the family

One hand held as a visor to their brows
they thought they could read a swallow
but it was only a frozen pebble and a rustling of feathers falling feet
    together

April didn't help their daily fare
Since they'd pulled up all the devil's grass
they ate an earth so cold their teeth became diaphanous

A hundred suns led by a thread didn't outshine their faces caught in
    the ice
They wrongly accused the layout of the walls
but the fault was an evil moon's which spat in their mirror

À J.-F. Auregan

Il la secoue pour faire tomber les mots qu'elle a volés
l'oblige à rompre ses fiançailles avec l'érable
l'attache à la même laisse avec une chèvre et un trèfle à quatre feuilles
puis lui donne en compensation la clé des champs

Il la renverse telle une outre pour la boire d'un trait
la hisse sur son épaule pour l'escalade de la pente
remplit sa bouche de gravier pour qu'elle soit comprise de la
     montagne
Il lui demande d'écouter sa douleur

Il traduit son cri en sept langues
mais musèle son écho qui fait sursauter le genêt
l'enchaîne à sa maison
l'y enterre
Il est si calme que l'araignée peut tisser sa toile dans sa tête

Chemin faisant
il croise un cortège de noces dans un pré
l'ange qui marche en tête tricote une brassière de ses cheveux
il l'invite au banquet avec sa coccinelle
mais celui-ci secoue la tête
sa charge est aussi lourde que son cœur

Le soir
il dîne seul avec son ombre
raconte au feu la femme l'ange le trèfle à quatre feuilles
sans dire à quelle époque remonte son récit

For J.-F. Auregan

He shakes her so she'll drop the words she stole
makes her break her engagement to the maple tree
attaches her to the same leash as a goat and a four-leaf clover
then sets her free in compensation

He upends her like a wineskin to drink her in one gulp
hoists her onto his shoulders to scale the slope
fills her mouth with gravel so she'll be understood by the mountain
He asks her to listen to his grief

He translates her cry into seven languages
but muzzles her echo which makes the broom-bushes leap up
chains her to his house
buries her there
He is so calm that a spider could spin its web in his head

On his way
he passes a wedding procession in a field
the angel walking at its head is knitting a baby's vest out of his own hair
he invites the angel to a banquet with his ladybug
but the angel shakes his head
his load is as heavy as his heart

That evening
he dines alone with his shadow
tells the fire about the woman the angel the four-leaf clover
without saying how long ago his story happened

Sa voix lui revient de la cage du canari depuis que le fleuve a bu son
　　champ et emporté son cognassier

Dos au mur
elle tricote face à l'araignée paisible
sa pelote de laine et la salive de l'insecte se dévident avec la même
　　lenteur

Le cliquetis des aiguilles elle le sait ne fera pas baisser le niveau de l'eau
n'attirera pas les hommes qui jadis enjambaient sa clôture pour
　　éprouver
la teneur en soleil de son rire et de son blé

Elle reprend espoir lorsqu'un ange s'échappe de l'horloge pour l'aider
　　à rattraper une maille

Her voice comes back to her from the canary's cage after the river has
    drunk her field and carried away her quince tree

Her back to the wall
she knits facing the peaceful spider
her skein of yarn and the insect's saliva unwind at the same speed

The click of her needles she knows will never lower the water level
will not attract the men who used to climb over her fence to feel
how much sun was in her smile and her wheat

She takes heart when an angel escapes from the clock to help her
    pick up a dropped stitch

Ses rêves lui font croire qu'elle est éveillée
un ange boiteux balaie sa cuisine
un troupeau de buffles est lâché dans sa lampe

Renversée la ville autour d'elle
persuadés de frapper à une porte ses poings martèlent un sol fermé
    à clé

Le rêve dit-elle est lieu de sépulture et de séparation

Elle rêve comme elle écrit
par hachures parallèles qui se rencontrent hors de la page

Dessine-moi un rêve dit-elle à sa main
qui creuse un trou et l'emplit de cris
Sa plume plongé dans les cris esquisse une maison
l'ange qui en balaie le sol a besoin d'un endroit pour y ranger ses ailes

In her dreams she thinks she is awake
a lame angel is sweeping her kitchen
a herd of buffalo has been let loose in her lamp

The town around her is turned upside down
convinced they're knocking on a door her fists hammer the locked
earth

A dream she says is the sepulcher of separation

She dreams the way she writes
in parallel slashes that meet beyond the page

Draw me a dream she says to her hand
which digs a hole and fills it up with cries
Dipped into the cries her pen draws a house
the angel who sweeps the yard there needs a place to put away his
wings

Assise sur son seuil en pierres sourdes
elle cherche la part visible de son rêve
face à la montagne qui gesticule dans le noir

Des hommes au corps froid incrustés dans ses murs
elle retient leur regard de reproche
et cette manière de renverser la tête en arrière
comme s'ils découvraient une nouvelle étoile
ou buvaient directement à la jarre

Leurs noms terreux jonchent ses draps bleuis par le froid

Il suffit d'éponger leurs ombres sur le dallage de la cuisine
et l'odeur mâle qui imbibe leurs vêtements du dimanche
pour faire reculer la nuit
vers le champ voisin

Seated on her doorstep made of deaf stones
she searches for the visible part of her dream
facing the mountain which gesticulates in the dark

Cold-bodied men are immured in her walls
she retains their reproachful looks
and that way of tilting their heads backwards
as if they were discovering a new star
as if they were drinking from a clay jar

Their earthy names are strewn on her sheets which are blue with cold

If she merely sponges their shadows off the kitchen tiles
and the male odor that soaks their Sunday clothes
the night will retreat
toward the neighboring field

Elle habite la chambre haute au voisinage des nuages qui la regardent
    trier les larmes et les photos
L'éloignement a durci les moustaches du soldat et fait gondoler sa
    dernière lettre
Elle se bouche les oreilles pour ne pas entendre les déflagrations
    lorsqu'il compare la tranchée à un paquebot
la guerre à un océan entouré d'autres océans

Il dit
l'oiseau transi qui l'observe est sa seule consolation
son chant et les armes ont la même stridence
et même pâleur novembre et ses poignets

Le verre fêlé de sa montre indique une heure à l'ouest
où les terres marchent à grandes enjambées
Les enfants gardent des maisons sans porte
Les parents dans leur fuite ont emporté la sainte image
Laissant sur le mur les marques noires de leurs prières

She lives in a high room next door to the clouds that watch her
    choose among tears and photos
Distance has hardened the soldier's mustache and wrinkled his last
    letter
She plugs up her ears so as not to hear the explosions when he
    compares the trench to an ocean liner
war to an ocean surrounded by other oceans

He says
the transfixed bird which watches him is his only consolation
its song and the gunfire have the same stridency
November and his wrists have the same pallor

The cracked glass of his watch shows an hour to the west of there
where estates walk in long strides
Children guard doorless houses
Their fleeing parents took the holy picture with them
leaving the black marks of their prayers on the wall

L'automne précéda l'été d'un jour
des jardiniers vigilants coupèrent plus tôt que prévu les cils humides
    de la passiflore
et les horloges tricotèrent des nuits plus étroites

Un vent jaune teignit les façades des forêts
les arbres cessèrent de jouer
et les balançoires pleines de fillettes et de merles s'arrêtèrent
dans un grand froissement de jupons et d'ailes

Novembre avait banni les larmes
des anges compatissants léchèrent les éraflures des petits genoux

Autumn preceded summer by one day
vigilant gardeners cut the passionflowers' damp lashes earlier than
    expected
and the clocks knit narrower nights

A yellow wind dyed the forests' facades
the trees stopped playing
and the swings full of little girls and robins stopped moving
with a great rustling of wings and petticoats

November had banished tears
compassionate angels licked the small scraped knees

Les morts dit-elle
sont clos sur eux-mêmes comme le sang
comme les glaciers
inutile de chercher leurs contours dans la vase putrescible des
    marécages
ou dans les remous concentriques de l'eau

Seules leurs voix traversent les obstacles
sans faire le tri entre ardoise et armoise
sourdes à la multiplication des cloisons
à la division du sol par l'odeur du blé

Leurs hurlements linéaires adhèrent aux parois lisses
miroirs vitres verres
Le tintement du cristal fêlé c'est leur désapprobation d'une terre
    pauvre en compassion et en soleil
le crissement d'ailes d'un coléoptère leur révolte face à la montée des
    hivers

Les morts
des travailleurs tardifs qui œuvrent sans serpe
sans maître
sans lanterne

Avec le seul bruit des branches
qui dessinent sur leur plafond des femmes ondoyantes
leurs bras de sycomore les enlacent dans leur cavité et font tinter leurs
    larmes

The dead she says
are closed in upon themselves like blood
like glaciers
useless to search for their outlines in the marshes' putrefying sludge
or in the water's concentric eddies

Their voices alone pass through all obstacles
without sorting blackboards from brambles
deaf to the multiplication of partitions
to the division of the soil by the odor of wheat

Their linear howling adheres to slippery surfaces
mirrors windows glasses
The clinking of cracked crystal is their disapproval of an earth lacking
    compassion and sun
the rustling of a coleoptera's wings their revolt against the coming of
    winter

The dead
tardy workers who labor without a pickaxe
without a foreman
without a lantern

With only the noise of the branches
which draw undulating women on their ceiling
whose sycamore arms enfold them in their cavities and make their
    tears chime

Cracher dans la pluie porte bonheur dit-elle
et elle appelle sur l'hiver les vents vieux et méchants

Car ce ne sont pas les étés qui manquent
les jours ressemblent à des généraux suffisants
les nuits à des femmes tapageuses
la lune est leur outil de travail
le régulateur de leurs pulsions et de leur sang

Mais il leur arrive de rêver d'un peu de veuvage et de ténèbres
Les grains de sésame cousus dans leurs jupes alourdissent leur ombre
sur leur passage les réverbères ont des inclinaisons lentes
et les lucioles écartent l'air des deux mains

Spitting in the wind brings happiness she says
and she calls down the wicked old winds on the winter

Because there's no shortage of summers
the days are like conceited generals
the nights like flashy women
the moon is the tool they work with
it regulates their urges and their blood

But it sometimes happens that they dream a bit of widowhood and
    darknesses
The sesame seeds sewn in their skirts weigh down their shadows
the lampposts bow gently as they pass by
and the fireflies part the air with their two hands

Elle portait son fardeau de brouillard par n'importe quel temps
L'homme qui planta sa maison plus haut que les fumées lui laissa sa
     corde à cinq nœuds

Cinq
comme les doigts nécessaires pour forer la tombe d'un moineau
lui rappela-t-il avant d'enfourcher le tournant

De son périple journalier elle apprit que les chemins s'étrécissent
     devant les villages pauvres
et qu'une seule cigale rendit sourde toute une famille de genêts

Ceux qui l'entendirent ahaner sous sa charge ne proposèrent pas leurs
     épaules glissantes comme leurs pentes
Ils ne connaissaient de l'étrangère que l'ombre verte qui s'allongeait
     jusqu'à leurs bergeries mélangeait enfants et bétail
puis traversait dans un éclat de rire leurs lits

She carried her load of fog in all kinds of weather
The man who set his house up higher than the smoke lent her his
    five-knotted rope

Five
like the fingers needed to drill a sparrow's grave
he reminded her before going around the bend in the road

On her daily rounds she learned that the roads narrow approaching
    poor villages
and that one cicada can deafen a whole family of broom

Those who heard her panting beneath her burden didn't offer her
    their shoulders which were as slippery as their slopes
All they knew of the stranger was her green shadow which stretched
    as far as their sheepfolds mixing up children and livestock
then crossed their beds in a burst of laughter

Il y a l'hiver dans son sommeil
les morts qui ruissellent sur ses murs oscillent entre bruine et averse
Elle se retourne sur sa couche pour changer de rêve
lâche les chiens pour faire fuir la pluie
L'arbre qui la pourchasse depuis l'orage baisse la tête pour pénétrer
    chez elle

Elle cache son cri dans l'âtre
sa nudité dans l'affolement des flammes
Sa robe qui traîne sur le dallage est rose de décembre
les souillures masquent un sang d'enfantement ancien

Elle dit non au platane qui réclame son humus
et dessina jadis le même vertige sur son ventre et sur l'aubier
liant son sort à celui de la forêt

There is winter in her sleep
the dead who flow over her walls go from drizzle to downpour
She shifts in her bed to change dreams
turns the dogs loose to chase the rain
The tree which has pursued her since the storm bows its head to
    enter her dwelling

She hides her cry in the hearth
her nakedness in the flames' panic
Her dress which trails on the tiles is pink in December
its stains hide the blood of a long-ago childbirth

She says no to the plane tree which demands its humus
and long ago used to draw the same dizziness on her belly and on the
    sapwood
linking her lot to the forest's

Elle dit
les migrateurs ne remplaceront pas la route
et ce ne sont pas les miettes de pain qui vont dérouter les hirondelles

Tôt ce matin
elle annonça au mélèze que son cerisier portait ses premiers fruits
Celui-ci le répéta aux autres mélèzes qui ébruitèrent la nouvelle dans
    la forêt
une forêt forte de son immunité et qui ne rend jamais les vents qu'on
    lui prête
elle les transforme en hurlements sous l'écorce
en galops dans les branches
en échos qui prennent appui sur la montagne pour se jeter sur son
    cerisier

Partir avec son arbre sous le bras est hasardeux
un ruisseau dessine un cercle clos autour de sa maison
l'eau enjambée tourne comme un mauvais lait

She says
migrating birds won't replace the road
and it's not breadcrumbs that will throw the swallows off track

Early this morning
she announced to the larch that her cherry tree had borne its first fruit
It repeated this to the other larches who spread the news through the
    forest
a forest strong in its privileges which never returns the winds it's been
    lent
it turns them into howls beneath the trees' bark
and into gallops among the branches
into echoes which lean on the mountain to throw themselves on her
    cherry tree

To leave with a tree under your arm is hazardous
a stream draws a closed circle around her house
once stepped across the water turns like bad milk

Le notable qui courbait la servante jusqu'à l'extinction de l'orage
est riche d'une seule mort
Elle appelle briques de malheur ses murs qui cassent les vents sur
    leurs arêtes
bouche édentée sa porte béante sur l'ouest

Seul le plafond est son ami
ses poutres lapaient sa peur au rythme de la gouttière lorsque l'homme
    la chevauchait dans sa sueur

Son fer à repasser plie en accordéon le drap frotté de haine et de
    prière
Elle chasse d'un geste de la main l'image de l'homme accroché à ses
    flancs
puis celle du chat qui mange une rose séchée

Les pétales à force de deuil ont l'odeur noire de ses aisselles

The dignitary who bent his servant backwards till the storm was
    extinguished
is entitled to only one death
Accursed bricks she calls her walls which break the winds on their
    bones
toothless mouth she calls her door gaping toward the west

Only the ceiling is her friend
its beams lapped up her fear to the rhythm of the drainpipe while the
    man rode her in his sweat

Her iron made accordion pleats in the sheet rubbed with hatred and
    prayers
She banishes with a wave of her hand the image of the man hanging
    from her hips
and then the image of the cat eating a dried rose

The petals have the black odor of her armpits from so much
    mourning

Elle dit
il y a un incendie sur la lune
les fumées de sable font larmoyer l'aubépine douloureuse

Un univers sans lune n'est pas crédible
c'est comme une tombe sans lucarne
les ténèbres mangeront les ténèbres
les océans feront main basse sur les champs
il faudra attacher les marais aux digues
tel l'âne à son piquet
pour les empêcher de noyer les poulaillers

Pourtant
elles étaient quatre lunes hier à rôder autour de son miroir
quatre venues avec leurs chaises rondes
pour assister à la levée du corps d'un ver luisant

She says
there is a fire on the moon
the smoke from the sand brings tears to the eyes of the sorrowful
    hawthorn

A moonless universe is not believable
it's like a grave without a skylight
the darkness will devour the darkness
the oceans will ransack the fields
the marshes will have to be tied to the seawalls
like a mule to a post
to keep them from inundating the henhouses

Nonetheless
yesterday there were four moons prowling around her mirror
four who came with their round chairs
to watch the body of a glistening worm be carried to the graveyard

Elle raconte ses rêves aux anges qui traversent son lit par mégarde
Une herbe froide recouvre ses draps à mesure qu'elle parle
"Alors que je traversais une prairie . . ."
Les anges qui l'écoutent bâillent poliment derrière leurs mains
    persuadés qu'elle se trompe de prairie et de rêve
qu'elle tricote avec un fil sans issue
au grand désespoir de son auditoire qui s'éloigne sur la pointe des
    ailes

She tells her dreams to the angels who inadvertently cross her bed
Cold grass covers her sheets while she speaks
"While I was crossing a plain . . ."
The angels listening to her yawn politely behind their hands,
    convinced she's got the wrong plain and the wrong dream
that she's knitting with an endless strand
to the great despair of her listeners who leave quietly on their wing tips

D'abord
elle tue la poule rouge qui trace des cercles autour de son champ
puis partage son œuf avec trois anges noirs

Elle décidera plus tard du sort des figuiers
quand le feu de septembre sautera de haie en haie en s'appuyant sur
    l'épaule des jardiniers

Ils sont deux figuiers à manger leurs fruits dans l'obscurité
à lancer les épluchures sur ses vitres
Celui qui a vue sur l'âtre raconte les colères des flammes
l'aveuglement de la suie
l'obstination de la marmite et de la femme à se vêtir de deuil
Ils la croient partie avec le chemin quand sa robe n'héberge que le
    vent
sa nudité taillée dans la lumière d'une lampe pauvre les rassure
Le duvet dans ses creux les déconcerte
Il provient du ventre du gallinacé qui tourne dans sa mort

First
she kills the red hen that traces circles around her field
then shares its egg with three black angels

She'll decide the fig trees' fate later
when the fire of September leaps from hedge to hedge leaning on
    the gardeners' shoulders

There are two fig trees which eat their fruit in the darkness
and throw the peels against the windowpanes
The one with a view of the hearth recounts the flames' rages
and the soot's blindness
the stubborn insistence of the casserole and the woman on dressing
    in mourning
They thought she had left with the road when her dress sheltered
    only the wind
her nakedness carved in a poor lamp's light reassures them
The down in her hollows disconcerts them
It comes from the belly of the fowl turning round in its death

Ses murs et ses os ont vieilli en même temps
Elle veille aux bons rapports qu'ils entretiennent avec le paysage

Sans son intervention
il y aurait plus de ronces
donc plus de disputes entre le vent et sa clôture

Elle mit du temps à croire que la terre tournait
C'est sa rotation qui arrondit les fontaines
les places
l'œuf
mais pas la lune
Elle a l'impression depuis ce matin
que la montagne s'est approchée de sa fenêtre
Elle marche sur les orteils de son pommier
pour la première fois il ne donnera pas de fruits

Her walls and her bones aged together
She tends to their good relations with the countryside

Without her intervention
there would be more brambles
and thus more quarrels between the wind and her fences

It took her some time to believe that the earth turns
It's that rotation which rounds off the fountains
the parks
the egg
but not the moon
Since this morning she has the impression
that the mountain has approached her window
She steps on her apple tree's toes
this is the first time it won't bear fruit

Elle pose son oreille sur le sol pour écouter les voix enfouies réclamer
    leur part obscure
elle les reconnaît à leurs cris enroulés dans des bandelettes

Parfois
elle arrache une dalle comme on soulève un drap
ignorant que ces voix ont migré vers la montagne pour remplacer les
    vents déserteurs

Les capturer ne lui vint jamais à l'esprit
leur présence incolore remplit ses mains
elle ajuste ses lunettes lorsqu'elle croit les voir dressées derrière la haie

Mais ce n'est que sueur de pierre
la trace écrite d'un lézard égaré
sa nostalgie d'un vieil écho

She puts her ear to the ground to listen to the buried voices clamor
    for their dark portion
she recognizes them by their cries bound up in mummy-wrappings

Sometimes
she lifts a gravestone as one would lift the corner of a sheet
not realizing that those voices have moved to the mountain to replace
    the deserter winds

It never occurred to her to capture them
their colorless presence fills her hands
she straightens her glasses when she thinks she sees them erect behind
    the hedge

But it's only stone-sweat
the scribbled trail of an errant lizard
her nostalgia for an old echo

Aux platanes qui regardent accablés le paysage elle comprend que la
  terre a froid
et ce ne sont pas les nuages loqueteux qui couvriront la nudité des
  falaises
Elle attend un signe du soleil pour se couler dans le chemin
qui mâche indifféremment le bruit bavard des pas
celui hargneux des charrettes

Le voyageur qui jadis partagea le pays avec sa valise remplie d'alphabets
lui apprit à lire le vol descendant des buses
écrit de haut en bas comme les firmans des sultans pourpres
comme les missives d'amour écrites au sang des violettes
qui pressent leurs pétales jusqu'à la dernière goutte
pour remplir l'encrier de la femme au ventre clos

She understands from the plane trees staring in shock at the
    countryside that the earth is cold
and it's not those ragged clouds which will cover the cliffs' nakedness
She waits for a sign from the sun to slip into the road
which indifferently chews on the talkative noise of footsteps
and the quarrelsome sound of carts

The traveler who once shared the country with his suitcase filled
    with alphabets
taught her to read the descending flight of vultures
written from top to bottom like the edicts of purple sultans
like love missives written in the blood of violets
which squeeze their petals to the last drop
to fill the inkwell of the woman with a sealed womb

Elle applique ses mains sur celles du pommier pour éprouver sa
     résistance au chagrin
Elle se sent responsable des blessures de ses genoux
et des sept lieues qu'il parcourut à pied pour se fixer face à sa porte

Elle lui apprit les vingt et une manières de marcher contre le vent
et comment se lever avant la lampe sans l'offenser

Il observa un mutisme douloureux devant la première neige
et les premiers cheveux blancs de la femme
convaincu que Dieu gaspillait sa réserve de craie

She places her hands on the apple tree's hands to feel its resistance to
    anguish
She feels responsible for the wounds on its knees
and for the seven leagues it traveled on foot to implant itself facing
    her doorway

She taught it the twenty-one ways to walk against the wind
and how to get up before the lamp without offending it

It kept a sorrowful silence confronted by the first snow
and the woman's first white hairs
convinced that God was wasting his stock of chalk

Elle dit
les noms des mois sont enfermés dans les livres
les gens reconnaissent les saisons au toucher
à l'épaisseur de leur sueur
à l'odeur mâle de l'amandier

La montagne peut bien s'en aller
à condition de laisser son ombre
nécessaire pour délimiter les frontières du vent

Il y a des neiges plus longues que l'année
des lunes plus vastes que la nuit
et des récoltes si abondantes qu'il faut mettre à contribution les oiseaux
pour séparer le grain de l'ivraie

Personne ici ne chasse les maisons à coups de pierres
et le jour pauvre qui s'arrête au bord du chemin bénéficie de l'aumône
    d'un juste
et d'un matelas déroulé près de l'âtre

She says
the names of the months are closed up in books
people recognize the seasons by their texture
by the thickness of their sweat
by the almond tree's male odor

The mountain can go if it likes
as long as it leaves its shadow
which is necessary to mark out the wind's borders

There are snowfalls longer than the year
moons vaster than the night
and harvests so abundant the birds must be asked to lend a hand
in separating the wheat from the chaff

No one here drives houses off with stones
and the impoverished day which stops by the roadside receives alms
    from a just man
and a mattress unrolled near the hearth

Sa maison lieu d'enfouissement d'objets muets
son jujubier stèle plus haute que sépulture de monarque
et comme la terre se mord la queue en tournant
elle déroule ses morts humiliés dans le sens de la marche
puis les assoit par ordre d'oubli autour de sa table

Elle leur sert des femmes en friche
leur donne à boire le jus de leur ventre
leur prédit de grands événements en insistant sur le rôle du jujubier

Ceux qui oublient leur odeur sur les murs sont renvoyés
Elle ne garde que ceux qui flambent avec ses sarments
font déborder les larmes de sa marmite
et ravivent les couleurs ternies du deuil

Her house is a burial ground for mute objects
her jujube tree a stele higher than the king's tomb
which like the earth bites its own tail as it turns
she unrolls her humiliated dead over her doorstep
then seats them at her table in the order in which they were forgotten

She serves them fallow women
gives them the juice of their wombs to drink
predicts grand happenings for them insisting on the jujube tree's
    importance

The ones who leave their odor on the walls are sent away
She only keeps those who flame up with her vine shoots
who make the tears overflow her soup-pot
and brighten up the faded colors of her mourning

L'hiver lui est douleur
lorsqu'une lune exiguë se déleste de ses déserts et de ses chiens sur la
    tombe du saint
qu'ils reniflent à la recherche de l'improbable porte
Sa préférence va aux loups qui enfument le paysage de leur sueur
    noire
laissant leurs traces sur les choses invisibles

Les loups dit-elle
d'anciens chiens humiliés par leurs maîtres
ils reviennent en visiteurs hargneux
justiciers maladroits

Parfois
ils disparaissent un hiver ou deux
et elle marque sa nostalgie en traits obscurs sur la suie de sa calebasse
jamais plus de deux hivers
le temps de disperser les vents qui aboient dans sa gorge
d'ailleurs ce n'est ni une question d'hiver ni d'été
mais de distance entre deux neiges et deux lunes

Winter is painful to her
when a narrow moon disposes of its deserts and its dogs on the saint's
  tomb
which they sniff around looking for the unlikely door
She prefers the wolves who make the countryside smoky with their
  black sweat
leaving their prints on invisible things

The wolves she says
are former dogs who've been shamed by their masters
they come back as quarrelsome guests
clumsy avengers

Sometimes
they disappear for a winter or two
and she marks off her regret with dark marks on the soot of her gourd
never for more than two winters
enough time to scatter the winds that bark in her throat
anyway it's not a question of winters or summers
but of the distance between two snowfalls and two moons

Pour Richard Millet

Il neige sur son lit depuis que son miroir s'oppose à la fenêtre
Bouger les meubles nécessite l'accord de la lampe qui rétrécit l'espace
Quand elle est mal lunée
la femme ne connaît pas le mode d'emploi des ténèbres
elle les refoule vers la rue qui les aligne sur un mur pour une
    exécution hâtive
et faire croire aux étoiles que la nuit est morte faute d'obscurité

It has snowed on her bed since her mirror contested the window
To move the furniture requires the agreement of the lamp which is
    shrinking the room
When she's under a bad-tempered moon
the woman doesn't know how to use shadows
she drives them out into the street which lines them up against a wall
    for a summary execution
and lets the stars think that the night has died for lack of darkness

La vieille a le deuil sourd de ceux qui vivent sur les pierres
ses défunts ne parlent qu'au vent en habitué du miroir qui les
multiplie jusqu'au figuier

La moustache du grand-père est une hirondelle qui boite de l'aile
La jeune femme morte en couches avait le soleil pour seul
interlocuteur
c'est à lui qu'elle souriait non à l'homme qui engrangeait son grain
après l'avoir emplie de glu

Ils sont huit comme les jours de la semaine qui ne sont que sept
dont trois enfants devenus anges qui n'eurent pas droit aux larmes

Huit à se relayer entre pénombre et lumière
leur ressemblance avec les photos devient visible quand le soleil entré
par effraction balaie le cercle du lit

The old woman has the deafened mourning of those who live on stones
her dead only speak with the wind as a frequenter of the mirror which
    multiplies them as far as the fig tree

Grandfather's mustache is a swallow that limps on one wing
The young woman who died in childbirth has the sun as her one
    interlocutor
it's at the sun she smiles not at the man who gathered his grain after
    having filled it with birdlime

There are eight of them like the days of the week of which there are
    only seven
and three are children become angels who weren't entitled to tears

Eight to take turns between shadow and light
their resemblance to their photographs can be seen when the sun
    breaks into the house and sweeps the circle of the bed

Dieu me pardonnera d'avoir laissé la maison s'éloigner dit la vieille
et elle tord ses mains en geste de désolation

La faute revient à la porte martelée par un forgeron hargneux
le cuivre retient les noms d'une seule syllabe
le loquet ne s'ouvre que pour les partisans des fortes pluies

Branches récalcitrantes et chevelures de femmes furent coupées d'un
    même coup de cisailles
couteaux et limes forcèrent des serrures fermées sur d'anciens bruits

Le sel avait sa responsabilité dans la séparation des murs et du sol
déposé dans la courbure du seuil
il rongea les pieds des défunts égarés entre sépulture et lit

Ils rôdent autour de la nuit
butent sur l'ombre des chaises
s'étonnent de se voir parallèles à l'armoire

C'est pour protéger leurs arrières qu'ils gardent la porte entrouverte
et pour l'inventaire des biens qu'ils muselèent les chiens qui tirent
    sur leur laisse dans l'arrière-cour

God will forgive me for having let the house wander away says the
    old woman
and she wrings her hands in a gesture of desolation

The fault is the door's hammered by a cantankerous ironsmith
the copper only remembers one-syllable names
the latch only opens for partisans of heavy rain

Recalcitrant branches and women's hair were cut with the same slash
    of shears
knives and files forced locks closed on ancient noises

Salt was responsible for the separation of walls from floor
placed in the curve of the threshold
it gnawed at the feet of the dead who lost their way between tomb
    and bed

They wander around the night
bump into the shadows of chairs
are shocked to see themselves parallel to the cupboard

It's in order to protect their backs that they keep the door ajar
and to inventory their possessions that they muzzle the dogs tugging
    on their leashes in the backyard

Elle mit des années à comprendre le comportement du vent
qui s'attaque à plus faible que soi
piétine des deux pieds le linge
puis le rend gémissant à la compassion du seuil

La pluie non plus n'était pas son amie
sa méfiance envers celle qui hachurait son miroir remontait au déluge

Le déluge disait-elle c'est avant la première page
quand les corbeaux étaient encore noirs
les hommes parlaient une langue incolore
les morts montaient à dos d'âne pour la traversée du rien

Le temps se suspendait derrière les portes
le feu se prêtait
la guerre se décidait à la lueur des lampes
la main s'emparait d'une braise pour signer un accord

Un monde d'une pauvreté paisible
toutes les terres étaient en friche
seul l'air était arable
le sol ne servait qu'aux femmes qui creusaient avec fureur
pour enterrer leur linge mort

It took her years to understand the wind's behavior
it would attack those weaker than itself
trample bed-linen underfoot
then deliver it up trembling to the threshold's mercy

The rain was no friend of hers either
her distrust of the one who crosshatched her mirror dated back to
    the deluge

The deluge she said came before the first page
when crows were still black
men spoke a colorless language
and the dead mounted donkeys for the journey across nothingness

Time was hung up behind the doors
fire lent itself out
and wars were decided by lamplight
a hand seized an ember to sign a truce

A world of peaceable poverty
all the fields were fallow
only the air was arable
the earth was only useful to women who dug in it fervently
to bury their dead linens

Si haute était la terre en ce temps-là
les femmes suspendaient linge et nuages à la même corde
des anges s'accrochaient à leurs jupes pour les empêcher de suivre les
    âmes égarées

Tout ce qui faisait commerce avec l'eau avait une âme
jarre calebasse bassine
les seaux repêchaient celles qui végétaient dans l'indifférence des puits

Toute ombre mouvante était esquisse de revenant
tout chant de coq se transformait en présage
l'annonceur des naissances parlait plus haut que la cascade
mais plus bas que le vent qui avait mainmise sur le dedans et le dehors
dilatant les champs pauvres
repoussant l'horizon d'un arpent lorsque les maisons s'étrécissaient
    aux dimensions des cages

Le sage évitait de croiser son chemin
il vous cassait un homme sur son genou comme une paille

At that time the earth was so high up
women hung out clouds and laundry on the same line
angels gripped their skirts to keep them from following stray souls

Everything that frequented water had a soul
clay jug gourd basin
buckets fished out the ones stagnating in the wells' indifference

Every moving shadow sketched a phantom
every cockcrow became an omen
the announcer of births spoke louder than the waterfall
but more softly than the wind which had taken over the indoors and
    outdoors
swelling the paltry fields
pushing back the horizon of an acre as soon as the houses shrank to
    the size of cages

The wise man tried not to cross its path
it would break a man for you over its knee like a straw

Quelqu'un parle entre les murs
mais personne n'est qualifié pour ramasser les sons
Les chambres du sud éventées ne retiennent que les phalènes
celles du nord fermées sur des roses nubiles préservent l'intimité du
    linge

Des femmes insomniaques y faisaient reluire les vitres avec leurs jupes
    retroussées
Elles avaient la fragilité de l'eau éparse
et la fiabilité du sang
l'anneau écarlate à leur ventre en faisait les maîtresses de la douleur

Un temps étrange frappait aux portes
il apprenait aux plus jeunes à lire la nuit
et à transvaser les larmes d'oreiller en oreiller

Someone is speaking within the walls
but no one is entitled to gather up the sounds
The musty rooms on the south side hold only emerald butterflies
those on the north closed on nubile roses preserve the intimacy of
    linens

Insomniac women polished the windows there with their tucked-up
    skirts
They were as fragile as dispersed water
and as trustworthy as blood
the scarlet ring on their bellies made them mistresses of grief

A peculiar weather knocked on the doors
it taught the youngest of them to read the night
and to decant tears from pillow to pillow

Allongée près de l'arbre qui respire à côté d'elle
elle pense au sycomore qui déserta son jardin pour se fixer de l'autre
    côté de la rue
Son ombre torture sa porte
le cri de la sève arrache des larmes aux battants

Et quand bascule la saison
il y a ce pas reconnaissable à ses semelles vertes
qui traverse la page de la femme qui écrit

Stretched out close to the tree which breathes beside her
she thinks about the sycamore which deserted her garden to settle
    down on the other side of the street
Its shadow tortures her threshold
the cry of its sap wrenches tears from the swinging doors

And when the season topples
there are those footsteps recognizable by their green soles
that cross the page on which the woman writes

Labourer la nuit fait perdre un pain à chaque sillon dit-elle
et elle éparpille les miettes sur le parcours du soleil
ignorant qu'il était soleil bien avant le sillon et le pain

La terre explique-t-elle était illisible à l'époque
à cause des vents qui l'effaçaient aussitôt qu'elle s'écrivait
de droite à gauche d'après les géographes de l'Aleph

L'homme qui communiqua avec l'âme du premier oiseau mérita le
    titre de musicien

Il n'y eut pas grand monde à l'enterrement du canari

Plowing at night means one less loaf from each furrow she says
and she scatters the crumbs on the sun's path
it had no idea it was the sun well before the furrow and the bread

The earth she explains was unreadable at that time
because of the winds which erased it as fast as it wrote
from right to left according to the geographers of Aleph

The man who communicated with the first bird's soul deserved the
    title of musician

There was not a great crowd at the canary's funeral

Elle eut une fois un livre
avec des lignes qui allaient d'est en ouest comme les trains de Sibérie
Une fumée noire s'échappait des pages lorsque les phrases s'ébranlaient
certaines se bousculaient
d'autres se laissaient enjamber par celles qui avaient décidé
d'atteindre le mot fin avant la nuit

C'était un livre d'intérieur
qui ne sortait jamais de peur que les vents médisants ne l'emplissent
    de tristesse
Il reconnaissait la femme à son odeur d'encre et de cumin

Elle riait avec lui
dormait avec lui
son doigt tâtonnant dans le noir de l'alphabet se posait sur le même
    rêve inexplicable

Un livre en loques descendait l'unique rue du village
le cordonnier ajouta une semelle à la phrase qui boitait
le forgeron lui offrit un fer à cheval contre le mauvais œil
et l'instituteur lui apprit les trois premières lettres

Elle fit un deuxième rêve trois nuits avant la grande crue
Son livre cousu dans un linceul attendait devant sa porte

Once upon a time she had a book
with lines which ran from east to west like Siberian trains
Black smoke escaped from the pages when the phrases pulled out of
    the station
some of them shoved each other
others let themselves be stepped over by the ones who'd decided
to reach the words The End before nightfall

It was an indoor book
which never went out for fear malicious winds would fill it with
    sadness
It recognized the woman by her scent of ink and cumin

She laughed with it
slept with it
her finger groping in the dark of the alphabet touched the same
    inexplicable dream

A book in rags came down the village's one street
the shoemaker cobbled a sole to a limping sentence
the blacksmith offered it a horseshoe against the evil eye
and the schoolmaster taught it the first three letters

She had a second dream three nights after the river overflowed
Sewed into a shroud her book waited in front of her door

Son linge trempera toute la nuit sous la lune qui lave à froid les cimes
    et les draps
À travers l'arbre dont elle ignore le nom le claquement du tissu éloigne
    les coyotes attirés par l'odeur rouge

Ivresse de l'homme qui a défenestré le corps nocturne
son rire ruisselle sous la lampe
le sang répandu est sa grandeur
sa brèche dans la montagne qui lui tient tête
les larmes mêlées de la femme et du grenadier

Grenadier répétera-t-elle demain en jetant l'eau de la bassine sur
    le tronc

Her laundry will soak all night beneath the moon which washes
     hilltops and sheets in cold water
Through the tree whose name she doesn't know the slap of fabric
     chases off the coyotes attracted by the red odor

Drunkenness of the man who threw the nocturnal body out the window
his laugh drips under the lamp
spilled blood is his grandeur
the path he hacked on the mountain that stands up to him
the mingled tears of the woman and the pomegranate tree

Pomegranate tree she'll repeat tomorrow throwing the water in the
     basin against its trunk

Entre le crépuscule et le pain fêlé
les mains de la femme sont deux pigeons de pierre
La fatigue les a fixées face à l'horloge adossée au mur comme un
    cercueil

Ses lèvres prononcent des noms connus d'elle seule dans un pays
de cascades et d'églises
où les saints servent la messe en chasuble de neige et
de prières venues d'un lointain alphabet

Parfois
ce frémissement du petit doigt
quand l'aiguille enjambe une heure morte
le chat sursaute
et la table chargée de silence éclate d'une soudaine abondance

Between twilight and crumbled bread
the woman's hands are two stone pigeons
Fatigue has immobilized them facing the clock up against the wall
    like a coffin

Her lips pronounce names known only to her in a country
of churches and waterfalls
where saints serve at Mass in chasubles made of snow and
prayers in a distant alphabet

Sometimes
at that trembling of the little finger
when the clock-hand steps over a dead hour
the cat jumps up startled
and the table loaded down with silence bursts into sudden abundance

Des rails enfouis sous les gravats
elle voit surgir ce train non inscrit au tableau d'affichage du vent
et que personne n'attend

Les hommes qui en sortent comblent l'écart entre les maisons
leurs voix élargissent les lézardes

Ils pourchassent la lune depuis la Grande Ourse
leurs lampes éclairent son échine
ses aboiements réveillent trois hameaux
trois clochers

Les chiens lancés à ses trousses reviennent le museau barbouillé de
     lumière

Ce ne sont pas les lucioles qui ramèneront le jour dit la vieille
qui vit passer le train les chasseurs les chiens la lune
et ouvre son parapluie pour se protéger des flots de ténèbres

From rails buried beneath the rubble
she sees a train burst forth which isn't on the wind's station-schedule
for which no one is waiting

The men who get off it fill the gaps between the houses
their voices enlarge the cracks in the walls

They've been chasing the moon since they left the Great Bear
their lanterns light up her spine
her growling wakes up three hamlets
and three bell towers

The dogs they set on her come back with their muzzles smeared with
    light

It's not the fireflies who'll bring back daylight says the old woman
who sees the train the hunters the dogs the moon pass by
and opens her umbrella to shelter herself from the torrents of darkness

Une odeur blanche de femme et d'été finissant les arrête
devant la haie
les trois murs
et le faux poivrier

Ils apportent le désordre au feuillage et à la robe de la femme
Elle les reconnaît au tintement de leurs larmes sur le parquet
à leurs ombres enrobées de sueur

Ils se fixent sur l'armoire à côté des pommes
font reluire le sang terni des cuivres
activent les feux du couchant

Trois murs avait la maison
le quatrième viendra avec la naissance de l'enfant

A white odor of woman and declining summer stops them
in front of the hedge
the three walls
and the false pepper plant

They rumple the foliage and the woman's dress
She recognizes them by the tinkling of their tears on the parquet
by their shadows coated in sweat

They attach themselves to the wardrobe beside the apples
make the tarnished blood of the copper pots shine again
light up the fires of the sunset

That house had only three walls
the fourth would come when the child was born

Elle ouvre sans réticence à la feuille d'orme sur son seuil
elle lira le message de l'arbre
une fois apaisées ses veines
et frottés ses couverts avec un mélange de cendre et de larmes

Elle sait les morts non impatients
et le myrte indifférent aux invocations du graveur
Que la terre soit ronde rassure son canari et calme l'eau de la fontaine

Le deuil annoncé par les nervures a pris possession de tout un
    alphabet
avant d'atteindre la femme qui fait pleurer son robinet
de crainte de diluer ses yeux

She opens her door without hesitation to the elm leaf on her threshold
she'll read the tree's message
as soon as her veins are appeased
and her silverware rubbed with a mixture of ashes and tears

She knows the dead are not impatient
and the myrtle is indifferent to the engraver's invocations
The fact that the earth is round reassures her canary and calms the
    water in the fountain

The mourning announced by the leaf's veins took possession of a
    whole alphabet
before reaching the woman who makes her faucets cry for her
for fear of diluting her eyes

À la nuit des coffres ils cèdent leur linge marqué aux initiales de leur
    bétail
Ils n'emportent que le cri de l'eau dans les puits
l'écho de la poulie
et des sangles pour retenir les vents impétueux

Ils donnent de leurs nouvelles aux troupeaux de nuages
qui paissent l'envers du ciel
buffles cotonneux effilochés par la tempête
boucs disloqués poussés sans cesse vers l'ouest

Ils se fixent sur les lèvres inférieures du pays
là où les marais font main basse sur les estuaires et les femmes

À défaut de chiens et de terres ils plantent leur blé dans l'écume
et dressent leur ombre à mordre les passants ombrageux

Septembre les plie jusqu'aux algues
ils sarclent le sel à la racine
puis l'envoient vers d'improbables meules

Lorsqu'ils se redressent ils voient quatre soleils de tailles différentes

In the night of boxes they give up their linens marked with the
    initials of their cattle
They carry away with them only the cry of water in the well
the echo of the pulley
and straps to hold back the impetuous winds

They tell their news to flocks of clouds
grazing on the underside of the sky
cottony buffaloes unraveled by the storm
dismantled rams pushed ceaselessly towards the west

They attach themselves to the country's underlip
there where the swamps ransack estuaries and women

For want of dogs and land they plant their wheat in the sea-foam
and train their shadows to bite skittish passersby

September bends them down to the seaweed
they pull up salt by its roots
and send it off to be ground on improbable millstones

When they straighten up they see four suns of different sizes

Le vieux qui ne sait pas compter
se sert des allumettes comme calendrier
et de la chute des noix pour agenda
De leur impact sur le sol il sait l'hiver tardif
il faut semer entre deux lunes quand les tabliers des femmes exhalent
    une odeur d'orage et de pierre brûlée

La voix à travers la fenêtre grillagée ne prédit rien de bon
son petit-fils ne jouera plus après les semailles
sa mère l'entendra courir sous terre
avec d'autres enfants
les jeux repris dans l'exiguïté des ténèbres seront ponctués de rires
qui feront redresser la tête au lilas

The old man who doesn't know how to count
uses matches for a calendar
and the fall of walnuts for an appointment book
From their impact on the ground he knows that winter is late
one must plant between two moons when women's aprons breathe
   out an odor of storm and burned stone

The voice coming through the latticed window predicted nothing
   good
his grandson won't play any longer after the sowing season
his mother will hear him running beneath the earth
with other children
their games taken up in that narrow darkness will be punctuated with
   laughter
which will make the lilacs lift their heads again

Le vieil homme qui oublia son ombre sur les rails
s'appuie contre un pommier

Il maudit trois fois la femme qui l'appelle pour piétiner son feu
elle grandit par temps d'orage et d'exaspération
ses voiles noirs se transforment en ailes qui ombragent la maison et la
    citerne

Lever son bâton pour la frapper
excite la hargne des corbeaux alignés sur le dos de l'air

Plus tard
lorsqu'il retrouvera son ombre
il videra la salière dans sa poche
s'allongera dans un sillon
tirera la terre sur lui comme une couverture
pour ne plus entendre la femme prononcer son nom

The old man who left his shadow on the tracks
leans against an apple tree

He triply curses the woman who calls him to stamp out her fire
she expands in times of storms and exasperation
her black veils turn into wings which shade the house and the cistern

Lifting his stick to strike her
excites the wrath of the crows lined up on the spine of the air

Later
when he finds his shadow
he'll empty the saltshaker into his pocket
stretch himself out in a furrow
pull the earth over himself like a blanket
so he can stop hearing the woman say his name

Le feu qui ravagea la dernière comète s'étendit à la châsse de la sainte
brûla l'ourlet de sa robe et le missel qu'elle lit depuis mille ans

Les anges analphabètes font la sourde oreille lorsqu'elle ânonne
    séparément voyelles et consonnes
leur rôle se limite à tourner les pages de leurs ailes
jusqu'au dernier balbutiement des cierges

The fire which ravaged the last comet stretched out at the saint's
     shrine
burnt the hem of her robe and the missal she'd been reading for a
     thousand years

The illiterate angels pretend not to hear when she stumbles over
     vowels and consonants separately
their task is just to turn the pages of their wings
until the last stutter of the tapers

On dit
qu'il a du sang aux ongles
qu'il étrangle à mains nues les chênes
puis noircit leurs squelettes sous son champ

On dit aussi
qu'il vient de derrière le soleil
où les fontaines meurent de soif
où les seuils mouillés se souviennent de l'eau

On dit surtout que sa maison n'est pas une maison
quatre pans d'obscurité dressés autour du rien
et le vent vertical en guise de porte

N'est pas son ami celui qui jette une pierre dans sa citerne
l'eau cassée fragmente son sommeil
et réveille ses chiens enchaînés à la colère du peuplier

They say
that he has blood under his fingernails
that he strangles oak trees bare-handed
then blackens their skeletons beneath his field

They also say
that he comes from behind the sun
where the fountains die of thirst
where the moistened doorways remember water

They say above all that his house is not a house
four patches of darkness erected around nothing
and a vertical wind making do as a door

Anyone who throws a stone in his cistern is no friend of his
the shattered water fragments his sleep
and wakes his dogs chained to the poplar's anger

Il raconte comme on pèle un fruit
le récit déroulé en un tournemain telle une épluchure d'orange

Même ses silences sont notés
l'écrivain public les transcrit en bâtons empruntés aux aveugles

Les oreilles de son auditoire étant de même taille
elles font le tri entre le vrai et le faux
suspendent le premier à leur plafond à côté des tresses d'ail
et jettent le reste aux chiens et aux mendiants

Les femmes qui l'écoutent emplissent leurs jarres de sa parole
puis le coulent dans leur lit lorsqu'il vacille avec la lampe
certaines qu'il parlera aussi longtemps que leur sommeil

He told stories the way you peel a fruit
his tale unrolled in no time like an orange peel

Even his silences were recorded
the public scribe took them down in wobbly lines borrowed from the
    blind

The ears of his audience being all the same size
they sorted out the true from the false
hung the former from their ceiling alongside garlic braids
and threw the rest to dogs and beggars

Women who listened to him filled their jugs with his speech
and spilled it out in their beds wavering in the lamplight
certain that he'd go on talking as long as they slept

Ils étaient trois à sortir de la nuit
avec le même nombre multiplié par lui-même de montures
trois silences à chevaucher neuf selles emplies de vacarme

Ils étaient riches en plumes et fracas d'ailes
leurs joues étaient soyeuses comme le ventre de l'olivier
leurs lèvres aussi rugueuses que son écorce

L'huile brûlait dans la nuit des sanctuaires
aromatisait l'herbe du diable
coupait l'acidité du premier lait
Les accoucheuses s'en enduisaient les mains pour arracher les enfants
    aux ventres des mortes
les gardes champêtres le répandaient sur le parcours invisible du colvert

C'était un temps d'opulence feinte et de gêne étalée
les banquets des notables croulaient sous le gel
ceux des bas quartiers regorgeaient d'invectives et de débris de jarres
Un temps de neige bavarde et de malveillance tue
la pâleur du soleil était le remords de l'été

There were three of them who emerged from the night
with the same number of mounts multiplied by itself
three silences to sit nine saddles filled with clamor

They were rich in feathers and the roar of wings
their cheeks were silky like an olive tree's belly
their lips as rough as its bark

Oil burned in the night of sanctuaries
scenting the devil's grass
cutting the first milk's acidity
Midwives smeared their hands with it to pull the children out of dead
    women's wombs
constables spread it on the mallard's invisible trail

It was a time of feigned opulence and flaunted discomfort
officials' feasts collapsed beneath the ice
slum banquets overflowed with insults and the debris of storage jars
A time of long-windedness and silenced spite
the sun's pallor was summer's remorse

Le vent dit-elle ne sert qu'à ébouriffer le genêt
à donner la chair de poule au renard
avec lui il faut consentir comme avec le diable

Vue de son toit
la ville avec ses maisons ressemble à du linge sur une corde

Elle n'eut pas d'enfants pour ne pas engendrer de morts
point d'arbre pour ne pas s'encombrer de son ombre
ni de murs
L'argile qu'elle pétrissait donnait un pain friable apprécié des serpents

Elle n'eut pas de chemin non plus
son ruisseau s'était tailladé les veines de chagrins entassés
et la Grande Ourse n'était pas praticable au mois d'août

Dans sa bassine de cuivre ses confitures bouillaient avec les étoiles

The wind she says is only good for tousling the broom-bushes
and giving the fox gooseflesh
one must consent to the wind as to the devil

Seen from her roof
the town with its houses looks like laundry on a line

She had no children so as not to engender words
no tree so as not to be encumbered with its shadow
and no walls
The clay that she kneaded made a crumbly bread favored by serpents

She had no road either
her stream had slashed its wrists with gathered grief
and Ursa Major was not feasible in August

In her copper bowl her jellies boiled with stars

Les enfants frappèrent à toutes les portes
pour annoncer qu'une cigogne avait accouché sur la plus haute cime
Le vent qui prend à rebours les maisons avec leur linge tiède fera
     tourner le lait de la mère

Ceux qui entretenaient des rapports amicaux avec la montagne
jetèrent du sel sur la pente selon le parcours immobile du cyprès

Leurs voix disloquaient les nuages
faisaient sursauter les chats non attachés

La montagne le cyprès les maisons sont de passage criaient-ils
seule la cigogne est éternelle
elle survole les marécages aveugles pour mettre bas si haut

The children knocked on every door
to announce that a stork had given birth on the highest peak
The wind which gets on the wrong side of the houses with their
   damp laundry will turn the mother's milk

The ones who were on friendly terms with the mountain
threw salt on the slope along the cypress's immobile route

Their voices dismembered the clouds
made all the cats jump who weren't tied down

The mountain the cypress the houses are temporary they cried
only the stork is eternal
she flies over the blind marshes to whelp so high up

Elle dit
la terre est si grande on ne peut que s'y perdre comme l'eau d'une
  jarre cassée
Contre le vent il n'y a pas de forteresse
le marcheur d'hiver doit compter sur la compassion des murs

Il y a des chemins hautains qui frôlent les agglomérations sans s'arrêter
d'autres plus modestes s'inclinent pour traverser les portes

Ils s'attellent aux travaux ménagers pour se faire accepter
se déploient dans les miroirs aveugles
se lovent sous la table à côté du chien

Elle dit
mais ne s'affiche jamais au bras d'un chemin
ne se montre pas au bras d'une route
et prend ses distances avec la nuit pour sauvegarder la blancheur de ses
  songes

She says
the earth is so vast one can't help but be lost like water from a broken
      jug
There is no fortress against the wind
the winter wanderer must count on the compassion of walls

There are haughty roads which brush up against towns endlessly
other more modest ones bow down to go through doorways

They yoke themselves to household chores to be accepted
stretch out in blind mirrors
curl up under the table beside the dog

She says
but is never seen on the arm of a road
doesn't appear arm in arm with a highway
and keeps her distance from the night to safeguard the whiteness of
      her dreams

Ils sont du même versant non de la même colline
issus de la même lune qui tourne sa lanterne trois fois avant de se
    prononcer

Leurs façades peintes en bleu c'est pour éloigner le mauvais œil des
    abeilles
les terres sarclées les jours pairs mangent les mains disent-ils
puis essaiment les maléfices dans le ventre des fiancées

Les filles riches de deux seaux ont droit à deux vies
une première avec un vieillard noueux
une deuxième avec un chêne intraitable
deux vies mais un seul toit
Ne possèdent deux maisons que celles riches de deux tombes
et de deux boîtes d'allumettes

They come from the same slope not the same hill
sprung from the same moon which turns its lantern three times
   before making a decision

Their facades are painted blue to escape the bees' evil eye
land hoed on even-numbered days will eat your hands they say
and then loose a swarm of evil spells in your fiancées' bellies

Girls rich enough to have two buckets have the right to two lives
the first one with a gnarled old man
the second with an uncompromising oak tree
two lives but only one roof
The only ones to have two houses are those possessing two graves
and two matchboxes

Il arrive à la forêt de se disperser
aux arbres de mener séparément leur vie
sur l'épaule d'une colline
ou sur la lèvre inférieure d'un fleuve

Les voyageurs les prennent pour ces phares de campagne qui éclairent
des morts nocturnes

Les jardins qu'ils côtoient les confondent avec les pèlerins et leur
lancent par poignées les rossignols

Dans quel sens tourne la terre
demandent-ils à ceux qui n'ont pas éteint leur lampe
prêts à suivre n'importe quel soleil

It sometimes happens that the forest disperses itself
and the trees go off to lead their separate lives
on the flank of a hill
or on the lower lip of a river

Travelers mistake them for those country lighthouses that illuminate
    nocturnal deaths

The gardens they frequent confuse them with pilgrims and throw
    handfuls of nightingales at them

Which way is the earth turning
they ask those who haven't extinguished their lamps
ready to follow any sun at all

Un homme n'est pas une île

Les miettes pousseront en arbre à pain dit la servante en secouant sa
nappe sur le jardin

Dans la chambre aux fenêtres béantes

la femme qui meurt compte pour la dernière fois les coups de feu du
chasseur

elle prend pour pétales la mie qui pleut sur son allée

pour supplique l'appel du rouge-gorge arrêté sur l'air

La tache écarlate de sa poitrine est son cœur retourné

Le sceau du soleil assis à l'intersection des branches

Il colorera le soir en rouge quand l'homme déballera sa gibecière sur
le sombre dallage de la cuisine

La morte descendra les marches pour l'aider à plumer la dernière
caille

A man is not an island

The crumbs will grow into breadfruit trees said the maid shaking the tablecloth out over the garden

In her room with its gaping windows

the dying woman counted the hunter's gunshots for the last time

she mistook the bits of bread falling on her footpath for petals

the robin's call stopped on the air for a petition

The scarlet stain on her chest is her heart turned inside out

The sun's seal is placed on the intersection of the branches

It will color the night red when the man empties his game-bag on the dark tiles of the kitchen

The dead woman will come downstairs to help him pluck the last quail

Les cigognes pondent dans le bénitier depuis que la maîtresse d'école
multiplie ses notes par les œufs puis les divise par les encriers

L'encens dit-elle donne le vertige aux cancres qui ne respectent rien
même pas la chasuble du curé capable de contenir tous les chats de
l'évêché

Elle fait bon ménage dans son placard avec les reliques du saint qu'il
sort en procession une fois l'an suivi des sycomores boiteux
Normal qu'ils boitent ils ont traversé l'évangile à pied

Storks have been nesting in the church font since the schoolmistress
   began multiplying her grades by eggs and then dividing them by
   inkwells

Incense she says makes the dunces dizzy they don't respect anything
   not even the priest's chasuble which could hold all the cats in the
   diocese

She arranges her closet to make room for the saint's relics which he
   takes out once a year for a procession followed by limping sycamores
No wonder they limp they've crossed the Gospels on foot

La caravane partie de Manama la vieille disparut entre Sirius et la
     Grande Ourse

Les protubérances du sable disent que chameaux et chameliers
     respirent sous terre
le désert s'affaisse
s'étire
se fissure pour montrer ses trésors pauvres
un bracelet de bronze pour la cheville de l'insoumise
de la poudre d'armoise contre le mauvais œil du soleil
et pour l'idolâtre un scarabée échangeable contre trois mules
trois filles nubiles
et une palmeraie

The caravan that left the old town of Manama disappeared between
    Sirius and the Great Bear

The hillocks in the sand say that camels and camel drivers are
    breathing underground
the desert subsides
stretches out
cracks itself open to show its paltry treasures
a bronze ankle-bracelet for the rebellious woman
powder of wormwood against the sun's evil eye
and for the idolater a scarab which can be exchanged for three mules
three nubile girls
and a palm grove

Sa préférence va aux années rondes
avec des mois qui tournent avec respect autour de son figuier
Sa méfiance des jours immobiles remonte à la dernière neige
les bras longs cueillirent les flocons nobles
laissant aux petites mains ceux des nuages inférieurs

L'hiver venu
elle se tient droite dans son ombre
un caillou dans la bouche pour empêcher sa parole de geler
et sa voix de parler plus haut que le vent

She prefers round years
with months that circle her fig tree respectfully
Her distrust of motionless days goes back to the last snowstorm
long arms gathered the noble flakes
leaving only those from inferior clouds to little hands

When winter comes
she stands upright in its shadow
a pebble in her mouth to keep her words from freezing
and her voice from speaking louder than the wind

Un jour dit-elle
je bâtirai ma maison de pierres et de lampes
avec ma tombe sur les branches
portée au bout des bras d'un sycomore

Des processions de pluies viendront la visiter
et l'horizon fatigué de faire le funambule sur une flaque d'océan
s'allongera sur son seuil

Je ferai la chasse au brouillard voleur de troupeaux et de silhouettes

Il marche en horde tels des loups incolores
égorge les ruisseaux
s'infiltre par tous les orifices
remplit corps et troncs de sa ouate
les transforme en cylindres insonores
ne laisse au sang que son écho

One day she says
I'll build a house of stones and lamps
with my grave in the branches
held in the outstretched arms of a sycamore

Processions of rain will come to visit it
and the horizon tired of walking a tightrope over a puddle of ocean
will stretch out on its doorstep

I'll hunt down the fog that steals flocks and forms

It moves in throngs like colorless wolves
slits the throats of streams
enters through every orifice
fills bodies and tree trunks with its padding
turns them into soundproof cylinders
leaves nothing but its echo for the blood

Why I Write in French

I'm a bigamist. I lead a double life under cover of writing. One day I'll write a book revealing the life I lead in the light of day with the French language and my clandestine life with Arabic. I move from the first, rigorous, meticulous, to the second: ample, generous in its leaps and gambols. It sometimes happens that I stir them into the same mold, melt the spirit of one into the form of the other, mix the colors of one with the flavors of the other. Arabic infusing its honey and its madness into French; the latter acting as a safeguard against overexcitement and sideslipping. The two of them are so mixed that I can no longer tell to which one this or that expression originally belonged.

Why, I've asked myself for years, do I stubbornly insist on telling my country's story in a language not its own? The answer is simple: living in Lebanon, I wouldn't have written books; I would have had children and cooked. The need to tell about Lebanon has come with distance. I needed to reinvent it as it was, divided, wounded, to give myself the illusion of sharing the daily terrors of my compatriots.

To write in those times amounted to an exorcism of misfortune, a transformation of the dead into characters, thus back to living beings. Novels like *Din for a Dead Moon, The Dead Cast No Shadow,* and *The Dignitary's Mistress,* published by Flammarion, and then by Laffont, served me as a mask behind which I could move through the fires which had emerged from my pen while my countrymen and -women walked through gunfire with uncovered faces. My country of ink and paper got the upper hand over the one of earth, trees, and water. I took shelter behind a white page while shells rained down on Beirut. What I made up had become more real than what had been buried under a weight of silence and omission.

A difficult time: I had to conquer the French language instead of taming it. The pen was my weapon, the white page the battlefield, and the constructions of Arabic the shield which protected me. A clangor of steel surged in my head while my pen made its way across the paper.

Cut off from my country and my people, I took hold of the French language, which had become at once my antagonist and my refuge, the source of my anguish and my certitude. To write in French amounted to writing without risk, without undue revelation, without danger. Arabic belonged to those whose terrors I only shared in pictures. The Arabic language belonged to those who died of it.

The idea so dear to Tabbouchi—writing as one's homeland—became completely meaningful. I was the citizen of a paper country whose geography I could undo or remake according to my needs, which I could populate with characters so unreal that none of my compatriots could recognize themselves depicted there. Homeland one carries on one's back like a nomad's tent to be pitched on more clement soil. Homeland shared with others astray between two languages, Kundéra, Castillo, Bianciotti, Ben Jalloun, Boujedra, Mimouni, who wander as I do in this French language which we wrongly accuse of rigidity and narrowness because it resists our convoluted sentences, our abundant adjectives, our plethora of metaphors.

"I must push back the walls of the French language so it can hold my own abundant tongue," said one.

"I set French up against Hungarian to put a distance between my terrors and my writing," declared Agota Kristof.

"I stuff the French language with loukoum, I teach it to do the belly dance," I added, so as not to be left out.

And this without taking into account the polemic provoked by Raphael Confiant's and Patrick Chamoiseau's discussion of the colonized reader upon whom the dominant and idolized French language is imposed. To all those spoiled children who break their toy and then cry for it, André Brincourt, in *French, Land of Welcome,* says this: "French does not become foreign as it moves away from its origins; on the contrary, it finds in these contributions come from elsewhere a music which draws it into the dance."

My real encounter with the French language goes back to 1957, when my brother, a budding poet, applied himself overnight to the alexandrine with the determination of a golfer to putt balls into the hole. He only wrote in twelve beats, only spoke in twelve beats, even when he was talking to his mother who must have thought the alexandrine was a descendant of Alexander the Great. When a line limped, my crafty brother added a syllable to resole it. To our neighbors, most of whom were illiterate, the phenomenon went unnoticed, but this wasn't the case for my fussy father. Was this tall boy with scraped knees who invariably answered him in metered sentences making fun of him? His suspicions became a certainty after he was summoned by the headmaster of my brother's secondary school, who questioned him about his son's poetic sincerity. What could he have been told that set him to observing his son with such intensity? He even followed him to the toilet, a toilet in name only: it was a latrine. The daylight investigations were followed by nocturnal searches, whose objective was anything exceeding eleven syllables. Any sentence with twelve was suspect. My sleeping brother was brutally awakened to explain the use of a past subjunctive, or of a noun converted to a verb.

"It was for the rhyme," he defended himself in a clumsy voice.

"Do I invent rhymes?" bellowed his progenitor. "And where would we be if I decided to invent sentences all the same length and the same width? Your sainted mother, your poor sisters, would have nothing to do but go begging in the streets."

Seeing that he'd gotten nowhere, he changed his tactics:

"What game are you playing, after all? Who do you want to impress?"

"No one," the defendant answered. "Anyway, I have nothing to do with it. I take dictation."

"Who dictates to you?"

My brother swallowed his saliva, opened his mouth, puckered it as if to whistle or to burp. Then, in a quavering voice, terrorized by what he was about to reveal, and at the same time ashamed of being an informer, he stuttered, "Victor Hugo."

Yes, Victor Hugo had chosen my brother and no other to whom to dictate his posthumous work. Years later, my brother would give over to me his pen borrowed by Victor Hugo to write in that French language, whose threads his muddled mind no longer could unravel. His stay in a mental hospital had made him forget his French.

This detour by way of Victor Hugo and my brother Victor is perhaps necessary in order to explain why I belong to that group which I call strays between two languages, to those voices which claim their due but are not vengeful, those writers who set language on fire for the pleasure of hearing it crackle, not as arsonists. I'd like to remind those pretended pyromaniacs, who commit acts of provocation because the beautiful is perceived differently in their mother tongue and because words sometimes don't stick to the object they're evoking, of what Rachid Boudjedra wrote: "As an Algerian, I did not choose French; it chose me. It imposed itself upon me through the painful history of the colonial night. But it's thanks to its great writers that I feel myself at peace in this language, with which I have established a passionate relationship."

"Francophone—like gramophone or Dictaphone," the playful Georges Schéhadé, who disliked the term, used to say. He went further in declaring that the word "Francophone" evoked an outlaw to him, someone wanted by Interpol, shown in a photograph handcuffed between two policemen.

The Francophone is someone who leaves a language he lives in for one which lives in him: that's my definition.

Books which guarantee a change of scene are expected of those writers classed as "Francophones." Parisian editors want folklore, the exotic, not realizing that, for me, come from the Middle East, the idea of wearing a powdered wig and lace neck-ruffles is the height of exoticism.

When I arrived in France thirty years ago, torn between my maternal Arabic, which helped me translate the French poets, and French, which wrote my own poems, I was incapable of choosing one of those languages over the other. They could be found side by side in my drafts: Arabic going from right to left, and French from left to right. The two joined forces at the heart of the page, and in my heart as well. Arabic, for want of speaking it, disappeared from my pages. I put on mourning for it when French occupied all my pages. Cruel epoch: I had the impression of having committed treason, and condemned myself to forced labor, producing and publishing novels and poems with all my strength. Alain Bosquet, who saw me at work, said

I had a convict's vocation. Curiously, my newly conquered language failed me at the slightest difficulty with bureaucrats or daily life. Bursting into a gas station one day, I asked the stunned attendant to fill up the tank and check the oil—in Arabic. To master a new language while retaining the old one requires a tightrope-walker's skill. It was not at all obvious how I could adapt French idioms to my internal structure. Nor was it clear how to create a link between two languages not related either in their solidity or in their porosity. Words added, words left out are the obligatory tax levied on the passage between two languages. I added and I deleted. In fact, I lusted after two identities and two ways of writing. I had become culturally walleyed.

"Francophone culture should not be created at the detriment of people's mother tongues," André Brincourt also said. "It should nourish them with new contributions, and vice versa. The French language has as its task to promulgate those languages which use French to recount other nations. A plural Francophone culture is rich in the diversity of the tongues which nourish it. Besides the French they share, Francophones employ a great variety of local and distinct languages."

"Can you live separated from the Arabic language?" I was asked one day. My answer is yes, given that Arabic lives within me, and that I insert it into the French language which is the tool of my trade. It is in the shape of my sentences, and in the mouths of many of my characters, since several of my novels take place in the Middle East.

Writing in Arabic by means of French doesn't prevent me from listening attentively to the latter:

to Racine, who taught me to tighten a sentence till it wept

to Pascal, from whom I learned to doubt the perceptible and to be sure only of the imperceptible

to insatiable Rabelais

to Montesquieu, geographer of thought

to melancholy Baudelaire

to Georges Schéhadé, the magician

to Céline, at once grandiose and base.

Vénus Khoury-Ghata is a Lebanese poet and novelist, resident in France since 1973, author of a dozen collections of poems and as many novels. She received the Prix Mallarmé in 1987 for *Monologue du mort*, the Prix Apollinaire in 1980 for *Les Ombres et leurs cris*, and the Grand Prix de la Société des gens de lettres for *Fables pour un peuple d'argile* in 1992. Her *Anthologie personnelle*, a selection of her previously published and new poems was published in Paris by Actes Sud in 1997. Her most recent collection *Compassion des pierres*, was published by La Différence in 2001. Her work has been translated into Arabic, Dutch, German, Italian, and Russian, and she was named a Chevalier de la Légion d'Honneur in 2000.

Marilyn Hacker is a winner of the National Book Award in Poetry and the author of nine books, including *Winter Numbers*, which received a Lambda Literary Award and the Lenore Marshall Award in 1995; *Selected Poems* which was awarded the Poets' Prize in 1996; and the verse novel *Love, Death, and the Changing of the Seasons*. Her latest collection, *Desesperanto*, has just been published. She is a noted translator, most recently of *A Long-Gone Sun* by Claire Malroux and *Here There Was Once a Country* by Vénus Khoury-Ghata. Marilyn Hacker lives in New York and Paris, and is currently Professor of English at City College.

She Says has been typeset in Bembo, a typeface produced by Monotype in 1929 and based on a roman cut in Venice by Francesco Griffo in 1495. Book design by Wendy Holdman. Composition by Stanton Publication Services, Inc., St. Paul, Minnesota. Manufactured by Bang Printing on acid-free paper.

Graywolf Press is a not-for-profit, independent press. The books we publish include poetry, literary fiction, essays, and cultural criticism. We are less interested in best-sellers than in talented writers who display a freshness of voice coupled with a distinct vision. We believe these are the very qualities essential to shape a vital and diverse culture.

Thankfully, many of our readers feel the same way. They have shown this through their desire to buy books by Graywolf writers; they have told us this themselves through their e-mail notes and at author events; and they have reinforced their commitment by contributing financial support, in small amounts and in large amounts, and joining the "Friends of Graywolf."

If you enjoyed this book and wish to learn more about Graywolf Press, we invite you to ask your bookseller or librarian about further Graywolf titles; or to contact us for a free catalog; or to visit our award-winning web site that features information about our forthcoming books.

We would also like to invite you to consider joining the hundreds of individuals who are already "Friends of Graywolf" by contributing to our membership program. Individual donations of any size are significant to us: they tell us that you believe that the kind of publishing we do *matters*. Our web site gives you many more details about the benefits you will enjoy as a "Friend of Graywolf"; but if you do not have online access, we urge you to contact us for a copy of our membership brochure.

www.graywolfpress.org

Graywolf Press
2402 University Avenue, Suite 203
Saint Paul, MN 55114
Phone: (651) 641-0077
Fax: (651) 641-0036
E-mail: wolves@graywolfpress.org